Using Relentless Empathy in the Therapeutic Relationship

With a refreshing approach to resistance in therapy, *Using Relentless Empathy in the Therapeutic Relationship* offers practical tools and tips to help therapists and clinicians across all modalities of counseling work with their most challenging clients.

By illustrating the power of empathic responsiveness coupled with attachment science and interventions, the author goes straight to the heart of what's vital for building strong therapeutic alliances with even the most difficult clients. *Using Relentless Empathy in the Therapeutic Relationship* presents effective tools that clinicians and therapists can use to move away from pathological diagnostic labels toward engaging with people in their distress.

This is a valuable resource to anyone in a helping profession, teaching them to effectively use their most valuable instrument—themselves—by harnessing the power of relentless empathy to shape relationships with not only clients but also the outside world.

Anabelle Bugatti, PhD, is a licensed marriage and family therapist with a private practice in Las Vegas, NV. She is a certified Emotionally Focused Therapist and Supervisor, the co-founder and president of the Southern Nevada Community for Emotionally Focused Therapy and the host of the videocast and podcast, *We Heart Therapy*. She is an author as well as a public speaker. She can be contacted through her website, www.DrAnabelleBugatti.com

Using Relentless Empathy in the Therapeutic Relationship

Connecting with Challenging and Resistant Clients

Anabelle Bugatti, PhD

First published 2021
by Routledge
2 Park Square, Milton Park, Abingdon, Oxon, OX14 4RN

and by Routledge
52 Vanderbilt Avenue, New York, NY 10017

Routledge is an imprint of the Taylor & Francis Group, an informa business

© 2021 Anabelle Bugatti

The right of Anabelle Bugatti to be identified as author of this work has been asserted by them in accordance with sections 77 and 78 of the Copyright, Designs and Patents Act 1988.

All rights reserved. No part of this book may be reprinted or reproduced or utilised in any form or by any electronic, mechanical, or other means, now known or hereafter invented, including photocopying and recording, or in any information storage or retrieval system, without permission in writing from the publishers.

Trademark notice: Product or corporate names may be trademarks or registered trademarks, and are used only for identification and explanation without intent to infringe.

British Library Cataloguing-in-Publication Data
A catalogue record for this book is available from the British Library

Library of Congress Cataloging-in-Publication Data
A catalog record has been requested for this book

ISBN: 978-0-367-68207-1 (hbk)
ISBN: 978-0-367-35044-4 (pbk)
ISBN: 978-1-003-13471-8 (ebk)

Typeset in Sabon
by River Editorial Ltd, Devon, UK

Contents

Acknowledgments — vii

Introduction — 1

1 Attachment science: The heart of life — 6
  Attachment basics 7
  Attachment: An integrated neurobiological system 9
  Secure and insecure attachment 15
  Myths about attachment 20
  What does secure attachment look like? 21
  What's your attachment history? Questions to consider 23

2 Relentless empathy — 25
  What is empathy? 25
  Views of resistance in therapy 29
  Relentless empathy and some uncomfortable truths 32
  Blocks to empathy: Countertransference 35
  To be empathic: The sponge vs. the mirror 38
  Final thoughts on empathy 40
  Questions to consider 40

3 Relentless empathy for resistant clients — 42
  Therapist resistance as a block to relentless empathy 43
  Client blocks in therapy 45
  Overcoming resistance in therapy 46
  Maintaining relentless empathy 48
  Questions to consider 50

Contents

4 Relentless empathy for personality disordered clients — 52
Personality disorders and trauma 55
Blocks to empathy for personality disorders 58
Narcissistic clients 60
Borderline personality disordered clients 65
Therapeutic directions 70
Questions to consider 72

5 Relentless empathy for addicted clients — 74
Addiction and attachment 76
Case examples 81
Hope for addiction 83
Questions to consider 85

6 Relentless empathy for angry or hostile clients — 86
Anger 101 87
The anger of hope vs. the anger of despair 89
Anger as a protector and advocator 90
The function of hostility 92
Violence in relationships 93
Leaning into anger 96
Practice activity: Leaning into your own anger 101
Self of the therapist window of tolerance exercise 102

7 Relentless empathy for difficult people in your life: Personal and professional applications for everyday life — 105
Authority figures need safety too 107
Using relentless empathy in the workplace 110
Relentless empathy on the world's stage 111
Directions for relentless empathy 113

Index — 116

Acknowledgments

"I can do all things through Christ who gives me strength."
– Philippians 4:13

Without the help of some very important people, this book would not have been possible. First and foremost, I'd like to thank Dr. Susan Johnson, founder of Emotionally Focused Therapy. Without her pioneering and trailblazing work, I would have never come to find my home and my heart within EFT, the counseling profession, and within myself. She has been a tremendous inspiration and mentor, and it is because of her that the term *relentless empathy* has a life. She coined the phrase and the practice of relentless empathy in her model of counseling, Emotionally Focused Therapy, and it has been life-changing.

I'd also like to thank EFT trainer Lorrie Brubacher, author of *Stepping into Emotionally Focused Couple Therapy*, for believing in me enough to introduce me to her publisher. Without her, this book would also not be possible. Thank you to EFT trainer Dr. Jennifer Fitzgerald for her writing expertise and for helping me develop my manuscript. I'd also like to thank my mentors in EFT who had a tremendous impact on my development as an EFT therapist: EFT trainers, Dr. Scott Woolley and George Faller. And in reality, this book belongs to all of the EFT trainers at ICEEFT who have each taught me something important about the practice of relentless empathy.

I'd like to thank my friend and colleague Dr. Dianna Troutt for your friendship, mentorship, and always being in my corner with love and warmth. And thank you to my EFT friend, gifted EFT supervisor/therapist, and facilitator, Michael Moran for your friendship and inspiration for part of this book. Finally, I'd like to thank my amazing husband, George, my mom for being my writing accountability partner and co-pilot for my writing process, and my family and close friends for their encouragement, support, and patience with me as I've gone through this process.

Introduction

This book is written for the book browsers out there.

Therapists are busy. We see lots of clients, we're attending training events, we're providing supervision, or we're receiving supervision. I would love to say that I have time to read all of the books out there, but I don't. I like books that I can browse and pick up some helpful nuggets without having to devote a few hours a day to them.

I hope that this book will offer exactly what therapists really need: a resource that is brief and to the point. I hope this book gives you some helpful nuggets without dipping into too many of those few precious hours you have for self-care. My main goal is to open your heart more than I hope to tickle your brain.

Let's face it. As a therapist (or clinician) in the mental health profession, we all have clients who are harder to work with than others. Some clients are more challenging to our own personal beliefs or personality, and some dig in and resist the help that we offer. It can feel downright uncomfortable and difficult at times. These types of clients are not unique to one particular setting for therapists. It happens across all kinds of environments in which a therapist might see clients. These might include mental health agencies, a substance abuse facility, a hospital psychiatric ward, and in private practice. Whether you see children, adolescents, or adults, you've experienced a resistant client who challenged your ability to be empathic with them.

Some settings may have a higher frequency of therapists seeing challenging clients than others. Still, no matter which setting we're in, we don't always have a choice with whom we work. We can't only see the clients who are fun, open to personal growth, and easier to work with. Even in our clinician training and masters-level degree programs, we learn to walk a fine line. While there are scenarios in which we need to refer out a client who is truly beyond our skillset, we are also taught that it is unethical to turn away a client simply because they're too difficult or "resistant."

As a mental health professional, there will be, from time to time, clients who we find difficult to work with. Some don't want to change, they resist anything that resembles responsibility for their actions, or they refuse or find it too difficult to see themselves as being part of the problem. I had somehow developed this false belief that in private practice, because you get more control over who you take on as a client, I would be able to weed out and avoid the difficult clients. Boy, was I wrong! I specialize in couples, so sometimes I not only have one resistant client in the room; I have two clients who may be difficult. Both partners might be digging in, seemingly refusing to work toward change, and then blaming each other, as both are lacking empathy and insight.

The field of psychology and psychotherapy has attempted to help us understand challenging and difficult clients through theories of resistance. However, these theories have not provided or maintained an active plan of approach as to how to help clients in their resistance achieve success in therapy. I believe this is mainly rooted in the history of the field itself.

The field of mental health began with psychiatry, though the earliest records of mental illness date back to China in 1100 BC,[1] and was treated with herbs and emotional therapy. Treating the mind emerged into mainstream focus in the early 1800s via the medical model, as most practitioners at the time were regular medical doctors. Psychiatry was the name given to medical physicians specializing in mental health. By the late 1800s, the field of psychiatry and mental health was well underway.[1] Psychotherapy, also known as traditional talk therapy, originated from Freud. Freud was a psychiatrist who developed what could be considered the first model of counseling, psychoanalysis. Thus medical practitioners founded the field of psychotherapy in the medical model of diagnosis and treatment as a disease, and the first therapists in the field were medical doctors. Following the medical model, psychoanalysis taught practitioners to leave themselves as people, out of the session. Freud believed that bringing the self of the therapist into the session would cause projections that didn't authentically belong to the client. In a way, he thought it would muddy the waters. So practitioners were taught to be emotionally disconnected from the people they were treating.

The field of counseling and psychotherapy has come a long way since the days of Freud. Yet in many ways, there is still some ground to cover. Out of the medical model, the DSM, the Diagnostic and Statistical Manual of Mental Disorders, was created to give medical practitioners a formal way of diagnosing mental disorders.[2] Diagnosing isn't all bad. In its most basic form, it helps the practitioner understand what they're looking at so they can formulate the best treatment protocol. Certain disorders came with specific protocols, which usually meant medication as the first line of treatment. Over time, however, the field of counseling, which is also practiced by nonmedical doctors, still largely uses the DSM to diagnose clients.[2]

The listed symptoms for each disorder are supposed to include contextual or cultural factors. However, I find that a lot of practitioners stop at the symptoms and don't really proceed further to the contextual, cultural, or attachment factors that may be driving the symptoms. In modern times, these diagnoses have become more like judgmental labels that even armchair psychologists throw around. Much of the time, they aren't being used to help people, but to judge them and put hurtful labels on them without really understanding what's happening in their world.

Sometimes we therapists may be inclined to label challenging or difficult clients with a diagnosis to try to explain such problematic behaviors. However, what I've learned from working with diverse clients and from my journey of learning how to practice Emotionally Focused Therapy[3] is that pathologizing people and calling them "personality disordered" doesn't offer a frame that feels empathic. Many of these actual labels have gone beyond a category once intended to help a person get proper care and instead have morphed into a way to label and judge. Personality disorders, in particular, have become synonymous with "resistant" and shorthand for "difficult to treat."

As I scroll through Facebook and see the many posts and blog shares from therapists, and hear horror stories from clients, I see that sometimes these labels are not a diagnosis with a proper treatment plan. These diagnostic terms have become labels of judgment about someone whose behavior can be hurtful and seemingly irrational. Stories with headlines like "7 Signs You're

Dating a Narcissist" and "5 Warning Signs Your Partner Is Borderline" are continually trending on the Internet. And I don't see just one or two of these stories a week; I see handfuls of them.

Clients have come to me with stories about how their last therapist said their partner was a narcissist or had a personality disorder, so they should leave the relationship. After I picked my jaw up off the floor, a part of me started to cringe on the inside. How on earth are these people identified as "narcissists," a clinical diagnostic term now turned into an ugly label, supposed to find help? Don't they deserve to be in a relationship too? How will they ever learn to be vulnerable if their own therapist is judging them or reluctant to lean into their pain?

Though not all therapists do this, I have found many who participate in the perpetuation of judgment. They casually use terms as labels without really taking the time to come alongside these clients and see what's happening in their world. The truth is, and I'm sad to say this of my profession, some of these diagnostic terms have become ugly labels conveying judgment, contempt, and a lack of empathy. Instead of helping them heal and grow, they are teaching everyone around them to "set boundaries" or leave the relationship. Usually, all that does is reinforce the underlying problem, driving the behaviors that got them these labels. If these terms are applied when a therapist identifies a client lacking in empathy, then certainly, the intervention for these clients should be empathy by the therapist.

This book offers a different perspective on difficult or challenging clients. The views of resistance are presented through the lens of attachment theory, and draws upon my extensive training in Emotionally Focused Therapy (EFT) pioneered by Dr. Sue Johnson.[3] EFT teaches therapists how to not only make sense of, but to also look beyond, the reactive behavior to the vulnerable person underneath.[4] Attachment is the framework, and empathy is the window in that frame through which we see and relate to others. EFT not only teaches therapists how to be masters of empathy but also how to be masters of Relentless Empathy.[3]

One of the reasons I love and practice EFT is that it captures the heart of clinical wisdom of attachment science more effectively than any other empirically based model. It really teaches us how to attune to those most sensitive buttons, the kind of buttons that are at the heart of our distress,[3] and are the most precious and important.

This book is devoted to the principles and practice of relentless empathy and the healing that it can bring to the most injured among us.

Details about case examples used throughout the book have been changed to protect confidentiality. It is my hope that this book will give you a new and refreshing outlook to help you see clients, and the people around you with a new set of eyes in a way that helps you both.

Notes

1 A History of Mental Health, https://en.wikipedia.org/wiki/History_of_mental_disorders
2 History of the DSM, the Diagnostic and Statistical Manual of Mental Disorders, www.psychiatry.org/psychiatrists/practice/dsm/history-of-the-dsm
3 Johnson, S. M. (2019). *Attachment theory in practice: Emotionally focused therapy with individuals, couples and families.* New York, NY: The Guilford Press.
4 Johnson, S., & Greenman, P. (2013). Commentary: Of course it is all about attachment! *Journal of Marital and Family Therapy, 39*(4), 421–423.

Chapter 1

Attachment science
The heart of life

> Over the lifespan, the need for connection with others shapes our neural architecture, our responses to stress, our everyday emotional lives, and the interpersonal dramas and dilemmas that are at the heart of those lives.
> Dr. Sue Johnson, *Attachment Theory in Practice* (p. 5)

Attachment is the essence of existence. It is at the heart of our humanity ... our quality of life.[1] The information in this book could not be understood without first understanding attachment and how it informs human behavior. As the quote by Sue Johnson above points out, at the root of human behavior is an attachment context.[2,3] When we understand the roots of a tree, it is easier to understand why the leaves look the way they do.

In this chapter, I will give you a nutshell version of what has been discovered about attachment and personality disorders so far. There are anthologies written on attachment science, so it is impossible to present everything. But hopefully, you will walk away from this chapter knowing the most important aspects of attachment and how it works. Because attachment is the bedrock of EFT and Relentless Empathy is the cornerstone of attachment, we will start with an introduction to attachment.

In the past, attachment has been widely known and accepted as being between children and caregivers but recently expanded to include adults and romantic partners as attachment figures. Much of what will be discussed is geared toward adult attachment because childhood attachment has a long history of more in-depth exploration and understanding. Also, most of the therapists I've met would self-report that it is easier to have empathy for difficult child and teen clients than it is for difficult adult clients. Why is this? Because, unfortunately, it seems that attachment implications for childhood behavior is more widely accepted than they are for adult behavior. Hopefully, this book will help bridge that gap, as attachment is something all humans need and experience, cradle to grave.

Attachment basics

What we've learned from decades of research on attachment is that attachment is no longer just a theory. Dr. Sue Johnson (quoted above), the pioneer of Emotionally Focused Therapy,[2] through years of research on adult attachment, has demonstrated that it is a science with empirical research and neurological data to validate and demonstrate its tenants and findings[4]. Attachment isn't just a science of love and bonding, but also a science of emotion regulation.[4,5] Additionally, attachment is a science of understanding human behavior, which makes sense when viewed in the context of attachment. The science of attachment provides a comprehensive account for understanding why humans seek and maintain close emotional bonds with others and why these bonds are so important. Richard Bowlby, son of Dr. John Bowlby, in his book about his father's work on attachment bonds, noted that attachment relationships are potent relationships.[1] Whether they are secure or insecure, they have a profound significance to the quality of our existence.

Attachment is a universal survival instinct; it is timeless and ageless, and its expressions may be culturally defined.[2,4] Humans are driven to be near the people they are attached to, especially at times of distress, and a close, secure attachment bond is our strongest guarantee of survival.[1,4] We are hardwired to seek contact, comfort, and connection with attachment figures.[2] As children, this contact is sought mainly through a lot of physical contact. In adult relationships, emotional connection can abide even when two people cannot be in the same physical space.[1,4]

In adult relationships, secure attachment is a reciprocal caregiving relationship in which both people are consistently emotionally available and present, emotionally responsive, and engaged.[2] As children, our primary attachment figure is our parents or our primary caregiver. As adults, a romantic partner typically becomes our primary attachment figure.[4] Those who are not in romantic relationships also describe close friends and family members as their primary attachment figures in adulthood. The quality of these bonds also matters. When the bonds are not stable and secure, they can become destabilized, distressed, and insecure.[2,4,5] If we don't receive consistent contact or the contact is not safe or comforting, the attachment system is not secure and may become distressed.[5]

Insecure attachment strategies can result from the lack of consistent caregiving or emotional responsiveness from our attachment figures. Abandonment, rejection, emotional cut-off, or isolation are some of the most traumatizing human experiences, and they can result in attempts to restore safety with our attachment figures.[2,4] The lack of secure connection with caregivers can rewire our neurological circuitry when we are young.[5] The good news is, because of neuroplasticity, we know that new neural pathways can be built, even later in life.[5]

Thanks to neurological brain imaging through the use of fMRI machines, we now know the brain encodes attachment distress as dangerous and painful.[5,6,7] If this distress remains a consistent pattern of interaction with attachment figures over time, a person will start to formulate a view of others as not reliable. Their ability to trust and rely on others emotionally, to see others as safe and supportive, will become strained and disrupted. Without healing or change, these patterns of distress can become rigid and generalized as a way of relating to others in an insecure way.[2]

Attachment also informs our view of ourselves and of others in the world.[4] Not receiving loving, consistent contact from attachment figures directly impacts the development of our self-esteem. Our ability to see ourselves as lovable and confident is directly affected by the quality of attachment care we experience in our formative years.[1,2] Our attachment frame is the lens through which we view ourselves and others in the context of the world. It impacts whether or not we see ourselves as either lovable, worthy, generally capable, or otherwise.[2] It's whether we generally see others as safe and reliable, or, conversely, as unsafe, unreliable, and having ulterior motives.

Our attachment frame (whether we have secure or insecure attachment) directly affects our ability to regulate our emotions. This is because emotions are routed through our nervous system.[6,8] How we regulate emotions outwardly shows up as our behavioral responses in the form of fight, flight, or freeze (our nervous system's appraisal of danger). These responses develop into our predominant coping strategies that form our attachment style: the set of behaviors we use to seek or maintain (or avoid) connection with others.[1]

Attachment also impacts our emotional responses and our behavior. Attachment signals are wired through the amygdala (the survival part of the brain).[6] Having a broken heart doesn't just philosophically feel terrible ... our physical brain tells us this is a painful experience.[9] This is why it's so important to work with clients in their emotional responses. We need to work with them on the level that their brain experiences distress to effect the most change.

Additionally, simply approaching therapy by logically explaining to our clients where things are going wrong isn't usually enough to effect lasting change. The logic part of the brain, the frontal cortex, isn't enough to talk our limbic system out of its appraisal of threat.[6,8] Most of the time, we aren't successful at talking ourselves out of our emotional experience because our emotions are part of our survival wiring. The logic center is a different part of our brain that shuts down when survival mode is in full swing.[8] According to our neurology, emotional distress is too compelling. When really understood, attachment culminates in humans through an integrated system.[2,3] It offers a way of truly understanding why people do what they do.

Attachment: An integrated neurobiological system

Thanks to technological advancement, attachment researchers have been able to actually see what happens inside the brain and the body during moments of attachment distress. Brain scan technology has allowed us to explicitly see that attachment is wired into our survival instincts. This technology has revealed the internal process of what we now know is a beautifully integrated system. This system functions for the benefit of our physical *and* relational survival and overall well-being. In many ways, it can be said that relational survival is part of physical survival.[2,4,6]

What researchers have discovered is that attachment is neurologically hardwired into our amygdala.[6] This part of our brain is also part of our limbic system that is responsible for survival instincts. It is the oldest part of the brain and has been present in even the earliest humans. Scientists discovered the emotion center of the brain in the late 1930s when they removed the amygdala from the brains of monkeys and found that they began engaging in really bizarre behavior, indicating that emotion regulation has a significant impact on our behavior.[8,9] This part of the brain helps us make meaning and emotional significance to the world around us. Basically, we are neurologically, biologically, and emotionally hardwired to bond with others.[4] Just as we are wired to scan our physical environment for threats to our safety, we are also wired to scan our attachment environment for danger cues that are threats to our attachment bonds and emotional well-being.[4,5]

Everything psychological and emotional is also biological. Emotions have physical cues in our bodies that help us tune into our experiences in the world and deem them as safe or dangerous. Emotions are our threat-detection system signaling the survival part of the brain.[5] When the amygdala detects an attachment threat, the pain center of the brain also lights up.[6] That painful feeling you get when you feel rejected is also happening in the brain. The brain experiences rejection painfully in the same way as if you had actually been stabbed—attachment pain is physical pain according to the brain.[9] Next, it arouses the nervous system, which propels us into action (a behavior) to protect our bond.[8] Our physiological appraisal, through our limbic system, of the world as safe or unsafe, is communicated through our emotions. How we regulate emotions then plays out in what we do, manifesting as our resulting behavior.[1] Attachment, emotions, physiology/biology, and behavior aren't separate entities; they are all interconnected in an attempt to keep us safe, to keep our relationships safely connected (hence an integrated system).[2,4]

Another natural process our brains go through is automatically making meaning of our experiences;[2,4] we have no control over this function. Meaning making is a survival mechanism that helps us evaluate our surroundings.[8] For example, if we see a snake on the ground, in a split second, our mind has already evaluated it as a threat. Then our body mobilizes our behavioral responses to protect ourselves from danger.[8] If we sat by that snake for a moment and tried to be logical (like saying to ourselves, "70% of the world's snakes are actually not poisonous. I might be okay"), we risk being bitten by the snake in the meantime. So we err on the side of alarm and see the snake as dangerous and respond. We cannot turn this process off or stop it, but we can harness it.

Like our hardwired survival instinct detects threats to our physical safety, this also translates into an instinct to detect threats or possible threats to the stability of their attachment bonds.[1,4,6] This ability functions similarly and automatically as our natural tendency to scan our physical environments for threats to our physical safety.[8] If we detect or perceive a threat, clued in by prior emotional experience, the brain neurologically encodes this signal as a danger cue. The amygdala comes online and fires off a danger signal. What we also know is the pain center of the brain lights up when we receive that danger cue. The function of this danger cue is to alert our body to move into action and avoid danger. The way this happens in the body is the amygdala arouses the nervous system, responsible for fight, flight, or freeze.[8] These responses become our mobilized behavioral strategy to cope with the danger cue—our behavior that becomes the way we handle this threat.

Our fight, flight, or freeze responses are the finite and predictable ways that we respond to potential physical and relational danger. In relationships, examples of fight responses might look like: talking more when another is silent, getting loud or angry to get heard, following when someone leaves an interaction or the room, pushing for someone else to talk about something, texting over and over (blowing up another's phone), not dropping a topic or conversation until it feels resolved, feeling your heart speed up or tension in your chest.

Flight responses might look like: getting quiet when emotion shows up in a conversation, clamming up, withdrawing, leaving the room, shutting down, yelling to shut things down, refusing to talk about a conversation until things are "calm," needing space. While freeze responses might look like: feeling frozen or paralyzed, numb, panicked and unsure what to do or say, not leaving a conversation but clamming up and not able to put words to thoughts or feelings, feeling confused and unable to make a decision.

Emotions are a natural tool given to us by nature to direct us toward safety for the benefit of our survival. The word emotion comes from the Latin "emovere" meaning to "move out".[7] Our brain prioritizes emotional signals, for the benefit of our survival, over logical solutions.[10] Our emotions move us to act; they compel us into action. Neuroception[11] is the term applied to the perception of our nervous system, the way our nervous system evaluates our environment and interactions for our safety or connection. This is the neurological term for the process the brain constantly goes through in scanning the world around us for threats.[11] This is an automatic process that does not require or involve conscious thought or intention to perform. When we aren't feeling threatened, our brain is able to engage our social engagement system which allows us to be more emotionally receptive and engaged.[8]

Whether it's our physical survival or the survival of our attachment bonds, emotions are essential and useful. Our emotions give physiological cues to our brain, appraising our environment as either dangerous or safe. We also know the brain encodes threats to our bonds as physically painful. Neuroscience also shows how the body physically reacts to threat, showing changes in digestive and cardiac functioning. These bodily responses also sustain themselves and often intensify when we do not process them; when we actively try to suppress them, keep them in, or ignore them.

Our emotions are data and information about our experiences, and they convey depth and meaning around these experiences in the world. Some people cope with chronic danger cues by using exaggerated, intense responses, and some do the opposite. Numbing out and disconnecting from our emotions is an adaptive survival strategy to cope with prolonged or constant emotional pain.[1,4] These strategies are effective in helping one survive, but when they are rigid and generalized, they are not effective in helping one build connection with others.[2]

In attachment terms, our fight or flight responses program our behavior to move into action to protect our relationship from breaking apart. It takes imperative action for the relationship to survive. This is the perfect system: neurological, emotional, and attachment form a trifecta that comes together to scan, detect, and mobilize into action to protect the survival of our attachment bonds and to help us cope with the pain we feel. When in distress, our emotions send a signal to our survival brain. Our brain interprets and evaluates the information, tells us when it's dangerous and painful, and mobilizes us into action to protect our relationships. The fact that we can now see this process happen in the body and the brain with advanced fMRI technology is exciting.

Our neurology and our biology are affected by our attachment relationships, a term described as interpersonal neurobiology.[11]

When people can be helped in understanding their emotional responses, they can begin to more clearly identify the message or need that is embedded in the signal of their emotional response. When this happens, they are more likely able to enlist their partner in more successful and meaningful dialogue around these cues.[11] When the couple can address the meaning of their emotional signals first, they can neutralize the threat of disconnection, and the nervous system will more quickly return to a calmer state, allowing our brain to resume logical functioning and come to a solution together about whatever the problem at hand is. This process is called co-regulation.[10]

When people do not get co-regulation, they are more prone to staying in a heightened state of arousal. Their body may maintain their fight or flight response such as stewing for days or needing to pull away and not talk for a few days or perform another task until their nervous system has calmed down.[10] Relational coping via co-regulation is far less taxing on the body and nervous system than individual coping.

The brain is also wired to prioritize these signals of disconnection so that we focus on healing our relationships above finding problem-solving solutions.[2] This is why, when couples get caught in conflict, they will often fight in circles and not be able to integrate logical solutions because their brain is under threat.[6] Most of the time problem-solving skills and logical reasoning are not readily accessible in this state.

The way we move through the world is significantly formulated by our visceral and emotional states.[8] As people become less and less connected to their gut feelings, their physiological being, there's less and less engagement with the realities of our external world in a less efficient way.[8,10,11] Because our eyes are pointing outward, we are externally focused (ever wonder what it would be like if we could focus our eyesight inward towards self?).

Think for a moment, have you ever had a gut feeling about something, ignored it, and then regretted it later? Why would the human body be equipped with these feelings, with these emotional instincts, if we weren't meant to use them? These are there for the benefit of our survival. Integrating these emotional signals helps us use the highest level of reasoning for survival.[11] More than just survival, integrating these signals helps us thrive in relationships and as healthy people in the world.

Yet when we avoid integrating the information contained in our own emotional experiences, or direct our clients to shut down or move away from theirs, we are doing ourselves and our clients a huge disservice. If we cannot connect to our emotional experience, our capacity to have empathy greatly diminishes. Cognitive empathy is nothing more than sympathy. True empathy is something we engage in on an emotional and visceral level.

Historically, the field of counseling and mental health has encouraged disintegration of emotional signals. When clients don't behave the way we want them to, the field has traditionally trained therapists to have two dominant responses. The first is to pathologize and label people as disordered, medicalizing their distress so we can give them a pill.[12] Emotional behavior was, at one time, even considered pathological. This was how the medical field approached humanity.

The second way involves trying to get attachment figures to set harsh boundaries or exit relationships as a way to try to control their partner's (or child's) bad behavior. We tell them, "when your child/spouse does this, you should do that" as a response. This is a type of behavior modification approach. Both approaches fail to get to the root of the behavior by pathologizing or trying to punish and control the behavior externally.[12] People act out when they don't have the language to talk about something that is inward.

Emotion compels behavior. If we don't get to the emotional and attachment root of these behaviors, whatever external intervention is placed on that behavior, the behavior is likely to continue or repeat itself (even if medicated). Intervening on behavior is like treating the symptom and not the underlying cause. Clinicians respond to the *form* of the message (behavior) rather than the message itself, which is emotional pain, and then wonder why it's not effective. A great example of this is if you flew to a foreign country where neither you nor the inhabitants spoke each other's language. You would have to communicate signals such as hungry, thirsty, or injured by acting it out. People act out when they don't have the language or the emotional safety to communicate what's happening inside. What people need is emotional closeness of a safe other to help regulate their neurophysiology. We cannot do that without being able to stay in a place of relentless empathy.

Secure and insecure attachment

Primary attachment figures provide an emotionally secure base from which one can explore the world around them.[2,4] They also provide a safe haven for one to turn to in times of trouble or distress for comfort and safety in the face of threat, fear, or danger. Bonds with an attachment figure develops based on the prevalence of experiences of comfort received during those moments, and we know that the quality of this bond plays a vital role in psychological and emotional development throughout one's lifespan.[2,4] Our relationship with our earliest attachment figures impacts the development of our sense of identity and self-worth. In an interview, one of our EFT trainers, Kenny Sanderfer,[13] so wisely said that "these relationships are the blueprints for our lives, and the ink never dries."

Insecure attachment results from inconsistent or unreliable caregiving, or a lack of emotional responsiveness from the primary attachment figure. This can lead to anxious, hyper-activated, or avoidant de-activated attachment behaviors. Insecure attachment bonds have also been linked to other serious physical and psychological problems, including chronic health problems, mental health problems, personality disorders, emotional and mood disorders, psychopathy, and even criminal behavior. Insecure attachment is also an important key risk factor in maladjustment to new or stressful situations and events.

On the other hand, secure attachment bonding comes from a reciprocal caregiving relationship and helps the development of healthy psychological resilience and emotional regulation. In securely attached relationships, each partner is consistently emotionally available, emotionally present and responsive, and emotionally engaged with their loved one. Securely attached individuals are more tolerant of differences in others. They have a larger capacity for sensitively attuning to others and effectively regulate emotions in a way that maintains emotional equilibrium. They also have confidence in their ability to handle novel and stressful situations. Secure attachment figures help co-regulate their loved one's emotional distress. "Co-regulate"[10] means helping them regulate their own emotions by being emotionally there for them. This presence is shown to have a calming effect on the nervous system, which in turn, once calm, can then help us focus on solving the problem at hand. We also know that a healthy and secure bond, the ability to securely depend on a partner to be emotionally there for us, fosters autonomy.[2,4]

Being rejected or abandoned in moments of need, distress, or physical danger can result in attachment trauma (because not all physical trauma impacts us traumatically). Canadian addiction specialist Gabor Matè[12] says that trauma isn't what happens to us; it's what happens inside of us as a result of what has happened to us. The quality of our attachment bonds plays a huge role in how we process traumatic events and what happens inside of us as a result.[12]

What's fascinating about attachment is that people can develop a mental picture of their secure attachment figure's soothing presence, and they can mentally access those loving feelings during moments of emotional distress, even when far away from their loved one.[4] Accessing the feelings around this representation can help them self-soothe during moments of stress and distress while away from their loved one.

We create, maintain, and manage distress through specific behavioral strategies that we use to either seek or avoid attachment with others, which are known as a person's attachment style.[2,4] Attachment styles are the behavioral coping strategies used to manage pain in the presence of relational/emotional threats. These threats are perceived or experienced threats to the security of an attachment bond, which can include disconnection from a primary attachment figure.[2] These strategies are used to seek or restore the connection to the attachment bond.

Attachment behavior is organized, maintained, and reinforced through attachment responses from attachment figures, and are activated in certain situations or terminated in others.[4] While attachment styles may remain stable throughout the lifespan, the definition of an attachment bond as either secure or insecure may fluctuate, depending on situational factors. Attachment behavior is not intrinsically pathological or childish. The security of these bonds impacts our caregiving behavior and our ability to explore the world around us securely.

Attachment styles or strategies are defined as either securely attached or insecurely attached. Insecure attachment styles are broken down into a few subcategories. In the simplest of terms, insecure attachment can be understood as either avoidant (de-activating responses), anxious (hyper-activating responses), or disorganized (contradictory attachment interactions with loved ones).[4] All three of these subcategories may be a result of trauma, either physical or attachment trauma. Disorganized attachment is usually indicative of trauma at some point in one's past.[12,14]

Those with anxious attachment styles have hyper-activated responses to attachment threats. (Remember, anxiety is just a fancy word for worry, and on an even deeper, more primary level, worry can often be traced to fear as well.) They fight for their connections by anxiously pursuing their attachment figure(s). They try to anticipate any and all problems, and then move swiftly into action to avoid these potential problems. Sometimes they try to repair a relational problem that doesn't even exist. Driven by fear of rejection or abandonment, those with anxious attachment strategies have a hard time trusting and believing that they are enough. When they make mistakes or hurt others, they have a hard time believing that others fully accept their apologies and that the relationship can be restored. They may do what I call "over-repairing"—not accepting or trusting that their initial apology was enough to repair the relationship or connection. They continually apologize and adjust their actions until the other person gets annoyed and starts pushing them away again. It's like they keep shoveling and shoveling until they dig themselves into a hole, and then they bury themselves.

Those that are anxiously attached can often become compulsive caregivers and insist on giving care and affection even when it is no longer appropriate. This can result in what some may describe as "smothering." This anxious caregiving is a way to help them create a dynamic in which they believe they are irreplaceable by others. They bank on the belief that their caregiving is valuable and wanted by others. This is not typically an effective strategy for getting secure connection.

Both avoidant and anxious attachment styles can develop from similar attachment circumstances in childhood, but those with avoidant strategies react to those circumstances very differently through inhibiting and disclaiming attachment feelings and behaviors. Remember, attachment strategies are also pain management strategies. In avoidant attachment, people will deactivate and deny their own emotional and attachment needs. This does not, however, mean that they do not desire to be attached.

Those with avoidant strategies tend to protect their hearts by avoiding allowing themselves to rely on others (out of fear of abandonment or rejection). They can become deeply distrustful of others in close relationships, and shift their behavior toward patterns of compulsive self-reliance. They typically engage in distancing behaviors as their primary strategy to cope with pain and distress, although their intention is to get distance from pain, not attachment.

Those with avoidant attachment styles will express less empathy and reciprocal support. A lot of times this behavior is a strategy to avoid perceived expected rejection and/or to avoid the pressure of being someone else's caretaker (being relied on or "needed" emotionally and/or physically). Even while desiring to be loved and wanted, this particular insecure strategy avoids being needed because of the threat of possibly letting others down or disappointing them. In a nutshell, avoidant individuals avoid relying on others, and in many cases, may avoid and reject any notions of being relied on emotionally by others.

An important delineation also needs to be made around attachment security. Attachment bonds can also be defined as secure or insecure apart from people's attachment styles. What this means is that people with insecure attachment strategies can still get together and have a secure relationship. For example, my husband and I both tended to be anxious in our attachment strategies. Someone who is more avoidant in their strategies will usually see an anxiously attached person (even securely attached people sometimes) as "clingy." But my husband and I had the same insecurities and used similar strategies to help us cope and manage these insecurities, so our behaviors didn't feel "clingy" at all. In fact, they just felt normal and safe. Our strategies helped each of us feel secure in the relationship. Strategies such as texting throughout the day, wanting to spend regular time together, or check-ins on travel trips felt safe and respectful. Maybe we can say we "clung" together. Though we both previously had been insecure in our attachment strategies, we were able to build a secure attachment bond.

Anxiety created by separation from an attachment figure is completely normal and not pathological in any way. Because we are relational creatures, separation anxiety is quite normal and healthy. Separation, however, does not necessarily describe physical separation. What helps couples maintain composure and security when physically separated from each other is emotional presence. Couples can be physically together, but one partner can still experience anxiety if there is emotional separation. Likewise, emotional presence can prevent feelings of anxiety when attachment figures are not within close physical proximity.

Separation anxiety is normal because it triggers the survival system to kick into gear to make sure the security of the bond is maintained. Anxious (and avoidant) strategies pervade when there is a lack of a secure base or secure base template. If a person had a secure base provided to them during their childhood, they are able to use this as their template or model of functioning, even when they are not currently in a romantic relationship. Relationships (a mentor, co-worker, lover, friend, therapist, etc.) are organized and assimilated according to a person's existing attachment model.

Secure attachment also impacts our physiology. When we are stressed or distressed, our body releases a variety of stress hormones such as cortisol and adrenaline. When we are able to get soothing emotional contact from an attachment figure during these moments, our brain releases pain-blocking hormones such as dopamine, serotonin, and even oxytocin. You could say that secure attachment is good for the heart, physically and metaphorically. Secure bonds help soothe the nervous system and regulate intense emotions during moments of emotional distress or disconnection. Having emotional contact with a loved one during difficult moments of stress and distress actually uses less glucose in the brain to process and cope. The brain and the body consumes less energy and also decreases the amount of cortisol and adrenaline (stress hormones) that get dumped throughout the body. These stress hormones are known to physically strain the heart and create a host of other health issues, including chronic health conditions induced by stress. Also, what researchers have found is that contact with a connected loved one during moments of distress can actually release pain-blocking hormones in the brain.[5,10] Connection can have the same calming effect on the nervous system as an analgesic (i.e., Motrin/Ib-Profen)! *This emotional contact is good for the heart! Quite literally!* (See Jim Coan's hand-holding study).

One interesting study asked people to rate their level of difficulty regarding the steepness of a mountain on a climbing expedition.[15] They were asked to rate the heaviness of their pack while completing the trip both alone and with a buddy. The study found that people saw the mountain as steeper and their pack heavier, when asked to make the journey alone versus with a friend, even though the friend would not be helping to carry the pack. This study helps demonstrate the importance of attachment relationships to our ability to regulate stress.

Myths about attachment

In his book, *The Making and Breaking of Affectional Bonds*,[1] John Bowlby's son, Richard, noted that his father had become frustrated by the reluctance of others to embrace attachment explanations for human behavior. Richard Bowlby surmised from his own experiences, that attachment science has a way of pressing our most sensitive buttons. It has the ability to trigger deep pain associated with memories we'd rather forget. He believed, and I agree with him, that this is at the root of criticisms of attachment theory.

Some critics of attachment theory mistakenly believe that stressing the importance of attachment bonding creates codependency and threatens independence. Let me be frank. This is false, and anyone believing this clearly does not understand the nature of attachment and bonding. I have found that 99.99% of critics of attachment theory genuinely do not fully understand what attachment theory and science is all about. They reject the idea that maintaining connected bonds has any significant impact on mental health. (I think this comes from the minds of critics with avoidant attachment styles.)

Additionally, dependence is a separate concept from attachment and is not necessarily related to the maintenance of closeness or connection and does not automatically imply an enduring bond. Clinicians, researchers, and society at large have assigned value implications to the idea of dependence that is in direct opposition to what it means to be securely attached.

Secure attachment is healthy interdependency, not codependency. Codependency is a form of insecure attachment. Healthy interdependence means both people in an attachment relationship can reach and rely on each other without avoidance or anxiousness, in appropriate and meaningful ways. Securely attached individuals are comfortable with closeness and their need for others. This form of healthy attachment creates a healthy balance between the self and others. Secure, healthy attachment bonding actually fosters healthy autonomy and independence. Anxious, "clingy" behavior or avoidant behavior can both be associated with codependency, which is not a part of secure attachment. Dependence on others is not codependency, and codependency is not consistent with secure attachment. Healthy dependence and independence are two sides of the same coin.[2]

> Secure attachment is healthy interdependency, not codependency, and fosters healthy autonomy and independence. Healthy dependence and independence are two sides of the same coin.

The more secure the bond, the more comfortable and relaxed people can be. The more secure they feel, the more they will allow themselves to explore, adventure, and try new things and develop their own identity.[2,4] But when people are insecurely attached, they tend to lack trust even if their partner did nothing to violate trust or boundaries. This may show up as suspicion or checking up excessively on their partner. They may get anxious or angry if they don't hear from their partner for a few hours. They may also get demanding or irate and have a hard time going to do any social activities. They may also struggle to feel relaxed and fully engaged and having fun with others apart from their romantic partner.

If partners are avoidant, they will go out of their way not to communicate with their romantic partner. They won't do any check-ins or make contact with their partner, and they won't communicate about schedules or planning activities together. They often don't let their partner know where they are or who they are hanging out with. They may also get irritated and angry, demonizing their partner as unreasonable or irrational for requesting more communication.

What does secure attachment look like?

What does secure attachment look like in a relationship? Securely connected partners are emotionally responsive, accessible, and engaged with each other. They have no problem reaching and reassuring each other, making emotional contact to prevent worry or panic, to give a signal of "all is safe and sound." Additionally, in a secure relationship, one partner does not immediately go into panic or suspicion or the worst-case scenario if they don't get a response from their partner. They don't obsess about what their partner may be up to when they aren't around. Therefore, the more securely they feel they can rely on their partner's emotional responsiveness and engagement, the more their partner is able to do their own activities. They can have fun without worrying about their partner tracking them, "blowing up" their phone, or pressuring them not to go out. Additionally, secure partners have no problem upholding relationship boundaries and do not take unnecessary risks that might threaten the relationship; they're less likely to play with fire (e.g., a married spouse going alone to a late-night drinking event with single, opposite-sex co-workers).

Secure partners have no problem helping their partner feel safe and secure. They are also able to exhibit understanding and empathy for their partner. For example, if they go on a business trip and they take a late flight, their partner might get slightly worried that their partner forgot to text when they landed. Their expression of needing reassurance, "I just wanted to make sure you got in okay," won't ruffle their feathers and send them into blaming their partner as being "so controlling." Securely attached partners would have no problem reaching out with reassurance and soothing contact for their partner, and in a secure partnership, their partner would be soothed by the reassurance and drop the subject and not feel the need to hang onto it.

Security has a balance between not demanding too much or spiraling into a panicked frenzy all the time. Securely attached partners are also not unwilling to verify, reassure, or keep in contact with their partner. *Secure attachment is a healthy balance between proximity seeking and autonomous exploration of the world.* And the more each person can trust that their partner is connected and committed and can trust them to respond consistently when they reach for them, the more each partner can relax and not worry about what their partner is doing. In attachment, this is called a secure base to go out from and explore our own interests in the world, and a safe haven to return to for closeness, connection, and soothing contact in moments of distress. In secure attachment, one can explore the world with increasing distance and time while making consistent contact with their base, and always sooner or later returning back to the base. Those who lack a secure base and safe haven are rootless and more likely to experience intense loneliness and depression.

Some may not know that insecure attachment is associated with mental and personality disorders and pathological and criminal behavior.[14,16,17] Attachment research shows that increases in attachment security are an important part of successfully treating disorders and rehabilitating criminal behavior. In short, attachment science says the help, maybe sometimes even the cure, for psychological and personality dysfunction is connection—securely connected, safe relationships with other human beings.

What's your attachment history? Questions to consider

1. Who could you go to in your family (as a child) for comfort or soothing? Whose lap could you crawl up on?
2. Would you go to this person for comfort or soothing? If not, why?
3. Whose approval did you long for the most and what did you have to do to get it?
4. Did you know you were loved? How?
5. How was love expressed in your family?
6. Was it okay to express emotion in your home with family?
7. Was it okay to talk about problems? Or was it encouraged to work things out on your own?
8. What did you do with your own emotions growing up?
9. Did you feel like you had a voice growing up? If not, how did you feel about not having a voice?
10. How was conflict handled in your home growing up?
11. Did you ever witness or hear your parents fighting?
12. How did you feel about them fighting? If you felt scared, what did you do to feel safe?
13. Is it okay to need others?
14. Do you view others as trustworthy? If not, how did you come to view others as untrustworthy?
15. What messages did you get from your family about love and relationships?
16. In your relationships as an adult, during conflict, do you tend to pursue talking about an issue and have a hard time doing anything else until the issue is resolved?
17. Or do you avoid bringing up issues, shut down, or withdraw?
18. What is it like for you when your partner expresses his/her emotions?

Notes

1. Bowlby, R. (2005). *The making and breaking of affectional bonds.* London: Routledge.
2. Johnson, S. M. (2019). *Attachment theory in practice: Emotionally focused therapy with individuals, couples and families.* New York, NY: The Guilford Press.
3. Johnson, S., & Greenman, P. (2013). Commentary: Of course it is all about attachment! *Journal of Marital and Family Therapy, 39*(4): 421–423.
4. Cassidy, J., & Shaver, P. R. (2016). *Handbook of attachment: Theory, research, and clinical applications* (3rd ed.). New York, NY: The Guilford Press.
5. Coan, J., Schaefer, H., & Davidson, R. (2006). Lending a hand: Social regulation of the neural response to threat. *Journal of Psychological Science, 17*(12): 1032–1039.
6. Johnson, S. M., Moser, M. B., Beckes, L., Smith, A., Dalgleish, T., Halchuk, R., … Coan, J. A. (2013). Soothing the threatened brain: Leveraging contact comfort with Emotionally Focused Therapy. *PLOS ONE, 8*(11): e79314.
7. Origin of the Word Emotion, www.etymonline.com/word/emotion
8. Porges S. W. (2009). The polyvagal theory: New insights into adaptive reactions of the autonomic nervous system. *Cleveland Clinic Journal of Medicine, 76*(Suppl 2): S86–S90.
9. Eisenberg, N., & Lieberman, M. D. (2004). Why rejection hurts: A common neural alarm system for physical and social pain. *Trends in Cognitive Sciences, 8*(7): 294–300.
10. Coan, J. A., & Maresh, E. L. (2014). Social baseline theory and the social regulation of emotion. In J. J. Gross (Ed.), *Handbook of emotion regulation* (pp. 221–236). New York, NY: The Guilford Press.
11. About Interpersonal Neurobiology, Dr. Dan Siegel, 2019, www.drdansiegel.com/about/interpersonal_neurobiology/
12. Maté, G. (2012). Addiction: Childhood trauma, stress and the biology of addiction. *Journal of Restorative Medicine, 1*(1): 56–63.
13. Personal Interview with EFT Trainer Kenny Sanderfer, Youtube.com/c/WeHeartTherapy
14. Brown, B. (2013). Brené Brown on Empathy. www.youtube.com/watch?v=1Evwgu369Jw
15. On Perception of Social Support; Scnall, Simone, Harber, Kent, Stefanucci, Jeanine, & Proffitt, Dennis. (2008). Social support and the perception of geographical slant. *Journal of Experimental Social Psychology, 44*: 1246–1255.
16. Bailey, C., & Shelton, D. (2014). Self-reports of faulty parental attachments in childhood and criminal psychopathy in an adult-incarcerated population: An integrative literature review. *Journal of Psychiatric and Mental Health Nursing, 21*(4): 365–374.
17. Mikulincer, M., & Shaver, P. R. (2012). An attachment perspective on psychopathology. *World Psychiatry: Official Journal of the World Psychiatric Association (WPA), 11*(1): 11–15.

Chapter 2

Relentless empathy

> Could a greater miracle take place than for us to look through each other's eyes for an instant.
>
> Henry David Thoreau

What is empathy?

Thoreau had it right. Empathy is a powerful tool of humanity, and can feel like a miracle ... especially when it comes to having empathy for those who we find challenging and difficult. Empathy is a channel of humanity that allows us to feel someone's emotions within ourselves. Drawing upon the work of Brené Brown,[1] empathy, in its simplest terms, is the ability to emotionally feel *with* someone by allowing yourself to resonate emotionally with their emotional experience. Empathy and sympathy are often used synonymously, and much confusion seems to surround understanding the difference between these two terms. One of the main reasons for this confusion may stem from the fact that different dictionaries define these two terms differently. The definitions seem to vary depending on what country the dictionary is from, and whether or not it's a medical definition versus a cultural definition, American vs. British definition. If you google search these words, you'll probably get bogged down in the litany of various competing definitions.

Combing through the convolution of dictionaries, sympathy seems to mean more of a somewhat detached concern for and an agreement in feelings for someone's experience. It may involve commiserating or feeling compassion or pity for the sorrow or misfortune of another. You feel bad for another, "I'm sorry you're going through a rough time." Sympathy is a good thing as it invokes compassion for suffering, however, it doesn't have the personal touch that empathy does. From my experience and training in EFT,[2] I've learned that sympathy is not the same as channeling a person's experience and feeling it with them. Empathy involves vicariously putting yourself in the shoes of another to help you feel their experience with them.[1] It offers a deeper way of understanding and being with the experience of another than sympathy.

Empathy means to allow yourself to access and resonate with, internally, the part of you that is familiar with the feeling being experienced by another.[1] Empathy is a skill that can be honed. It allows you to touch and access an emotional muscle memory, the part of you that remembers what it's like to feel that way, in a way that brings you into deeper understanding of the experience of another. People can feel when you're with them, and they can feel when you're not. It's not something you can necessarily explain from a mental place; it's a felt sense, and we all know when we feel someone's emotional presence, and when we don't. This could be someone telling you they don't think you get it, even though you're trying to convey that you do, and on a mental level, you totally might get them. But what they're really saying is they don't feel your presence in that emotional space with them.

Heinz Kohut was one of the first practitioners to write about empathy in psychotherapy.[3] Though ironically, he was a psychoanalyst, the model of therapy that I would say had the *least* emphasis on empathy, Kohut wrote about what he thought empathy was and what it was not. In his writings, he theorized that empathy could primarily be used as a way to understand and explain what the therapist has observed,[3] but not as a way of relating to the client and building a strong therapeutic alliance with them.

Kohut didn't seem to recognize that empathy is more than just cognitive understanding; it is emotional. It means I can emotionally understand you in a deep and meaningful way. It doesn't mean that I can just relate to your thoughts; it means on some level I can feel with you. It doesn't necessarily mean that our felt experience is exactly the same as our clients. It means that we can access the part of our emotions that is familiar with the feeling.

Where Kohut and other great contributors to our knowledge of empathy stopped short was in seeing the ability of empathy to help shape the therapeutic alliance. We know from attachment science and research that the definition of an attachment bond as secure or insecure has *plasticity*: it can change and be shaped. When clients come to therapy, they do form an attachment bond with their therapist. It may not be a bond that goes beyond the therapeutic relationship, but this relationship, in many cases, may be the only safe attachment bond our clients have ever experienced. Think about it for a moment. When our clients come into our room, we are strangers to them. Yet they are expected to be willing to be open about some of the most vulnerable and personal details of their private lives. People cannot do these things if they sense or fear they will be rejected or judged. Emotional safety cannot be built without empathy. Safety is the preamble to attachment after all.

Empathy is different from sympathy. Sympathy is feeling *something similar by entering your own experience* without really entering into the other's specific emotional experience.[1] Empathy is also different than simply cognitively understanding someone, which feels more detached. First and foremost, empathy requires the ability to be emotionally present and to feel emotion. Furthermore, it requires the ability to enter into someone else's emotional experience. The person conveying empathy then becomes like an emotional resonating chamber, allowing the emotion to echo through them and back to the other person as they enter into their specific emotional experience, reflecting the felt sense of a shared emotional state with another. If we cannot feel emotions, or we do not allow ourselves to feel emotions, we cannot fully enter the emotional experience of another. Thus, we cannot fully have empathy, period. The person showing empathy has to allow themselves to go to that emotional depth within themselves in order to emotionally resonate with the other person.

Think of empathy as understanding someone by allowing yourself to access the emotional memory of the presented emotion within you. Allow yourself to touch the place inside that emotionally remembers what that feeling, that emotional place, is like to be in. Then reflect it back to the other person as a way to join and connect with them where they're at. When we emotionally join with another—connect on an emotional level—that individual feels deeply seen, understood, and, most importantly, they don't feel alone in their emotions. They don't feel alone in their pain.

People long to feel like they aren't the only one feeling what they feel, that they aren't broken or dysfunctional for feeling that way. Not feeling alone in their pain helps lighten the emotional load, literally. Neuroscience has shown that this actually helps have a calming effect on the nervous system. Connection with others helps the nervous system better regulate itself and lighten the amount of stress hormones released into the body. It's a big relief to know that we're not alone in feeling a certain way, that others feel that way too.

This connection surpasses just mentally understanding them and transcends to a deeper level that transforms the relationship, allowing a deeper level of connection and emotional safety. But we don't have to get weighed down by the emotion in order to be fully emotionally present and empathic with them. This is a concern I've heard some therapists convey. Their worry is that emotionally joining with the other will leave them feeling drained, depleted, or weighed down. Empathizing, to them, means being dragged down into depths they don't want to go into. And in some ways, they're right. They don't fully understand that empathy is a willingness to go into those places without fear. Therapists must remember that at the end of the day, it's about being with the other person.

With true empathy, no one is dragging you to that place; it's a choice you make. And if you're not willing to go there, you won't be able to convey true empathy. You may be able to convey sympathy, which is a form of compassion. But you won't be able to truly convey empathy, and the client will feel it. True empathy requires emotional courage. Are you willing to brave the storm of painful emotions with another person? Will you walk with them in their pain? It doesn't mean you absorb their pain; you can empathize with someone without absorbing their emotional state. (We'll go into this in more detail later.)

At the heart of it, empathy is always about the other person and in the service of the relationship. It's a relationship-building skill. It's a building block of secure human bonding and connection. However, sometimes, we get blocked from being able to empathize with others. Blocks are anything that gets in the way of, limits, inhibits, or prevents us from being able to do something. Sometimes it's our own stuff that gets in the way. Our goal may be to empathize with another, but if we haven't healed our own wounds or gotten our own needs for connection met, as we touch those emotional places in ourselves, we might get hijacked into our own emotions or experience. When that happens, it's no longer about the other person; the spotlight is on us. It's not really empathy at that moment. It's shifted away from empathy because we're not fully present with them when we're in our own experience.

Empathy can also get blocked when we feel clients dig in to their defenses and behaviors, and seem to be resistant to any of our suggestions. They may emotionally protest, act out, avoid, or do anything or everything except go where we're asking them to go emotionally. This can be frustrating for therapists, and sometimes those defenses and avoidance strategies can trigger deeper feelings inside of the therapist, hijacking their presence again. Therapists can get caught up in their own thoughts of "why is this client being so difficult?" or feeling fearful that maybe a better therapist would be able to get the client to cooperate. The therapist may not realize that the client's resistance is about their own pain, and not necessarily about the skills of the therapist. This is why I have found that the attachment view of resistance offers the easiest and most grounding path back into empathy for clients.

Views of resistance in therapy

Most theories of resistance in psychology or counseling conceptualize resistance of a client as an unwillingness to grow or change their behavior in therapy, or an unwillingness to receive input from the therapist.[4] Resistance can be considered a defense mechanism, but why the defenses are up is where the therapist's own understanding of what's happening can stray from the path of empathy. Some modalities of counseling offer narrow views of resistance. Many of them centering around finding some pathology within the client and treating them as the problem rather than an equally important party *with* a problem.

What I've learned about pathologizing or diagnosing resistance as a mental disorder or a personality disorder, is that it doesn't actually lend itself to helping the therapist find a treatment that will effect change (healing and growing). It also tends to invalidate the client's human experience and sends them an emotional message that their pain doesn't matter, won't be heard, and that they are broken and dysfunctional and need to be medicated for the way they are dealing with problems at hand.

In Emotionally Focused Therapy (EFT), our stance is always through the attachment frame.[2] Remember that attachment science offers us a way of understanding human behavior, including resistance. According to EFT and attachment, the client isn't digging in because they're sick or stubborn; it's because they're in pain or scared, they don't know how to do it another way, or they're insecure in their abilities to try something emotionally new and risky.[2]

When we remember that attachment literally is a survival instinct, and that emotion is wired through our nervous system as our body's physiological way of moving into action (behavior) to survive and protect our relationships, then it makes much more sense why people do what they do and respond the way that they do. The less connected and self-aware someone is, the more random they may believe their behavior or emotion. It's not random at all, in fact, it's quite predictable, as there's only a finite set of ways of responding to a stimulus; fight, flight or freeze. Someone who says their emotions or behavior seem random are really saying they're not in tune at all, and not connected to their own body's system of emotional signals and how they respond to that information. By also recognizing how predictable human responses and behaviors are, and that no behavior on earth is without some emotional motivating factor, it helps remove the pathology, stigma, and fear out of emotion and helps put us back in the control seat of getting in tune with the emotional signals, gleaning the information they're presenting, and learning how to do something better with that information.

When we try to use an intervention in therapy, and the client struggles to cooperate or seems unwilling to, most often, it's because we've asked them to do something they're not ready to do, or we've asked them to bite off a bigger chunk than they can chew. Recognizing this can take us from the path of judgment to a place of empathy. I love EFT and attachment because they free us from judgment and puts us back at the heart of the human condition. In EFT, we say that resistance is valuable information. If the client does what you ask them to do, *great!* If they don't do what you ask them to do, that's great too. It means that we've hit something important, though it may feel bumpy and rough. In some ways, we've struck emotional oil there because we know we've hit a place of fear or pain. This is a valuable key to the client's emotional experience, and, in EFT, we're good at leaning in and getting curious.

Perception is reality. It is literally the way our body interprets and makes meaning out of the information and stimuli from the outside world. This is an automatic process and that cannot be stopped. And while reality may be subjective, many people get caught in the trap of trying to talk another out of their reality instead of leaning into their own or someone else's reality and getting curious about what signals are coming in that are resulting in that feeling and response. The reality we experience may not always be the desired reality, and often times it is different than the reality of someone else's reality. Many people in relationships experience distress and conflict around a clash of different realities. Again, maybe the reality I'm experiencing or that my partner is experiencing is not the reality I'm wanting to experience, or not how I want that other person to experience me. But the logic center of my brain literally cannot talk our nervous system out of this experience. This is where many people get stuck and not able to make a change. If we can lean into each other's realities and understand the information signals (meaning and emotions), then we can better understand what's happening for ourselves and each other, and work together on finding a solution for co-creating a new reality that is in tune and aligned with our shared goals and longings for connection and success.

Most importantly, relentless empathy helps us move away from pathology and back into humanness. Even when a client says they don't feel emotions, there's a reason. Don't be fooled. No one is a robot completely devoid of feeling, even though they may do a good job at convincing you and themselves of it. Remember that attachment teaches us there's always a reason for the behavior and emotional responses (or lack thereof). Not feeling is an emotional survival strategy. To emotionally numb out is a way to protect one's self from emotional danger or hurt. Usually, people don't start numbing out because they're feeling blissful. They numb out because something is painful. They've probably been rejected, abandoned, or emotionally whacked enough to know they're hurting, and numbing out the hurt is the only way they can move on. When you see an emotionless client, don't be fooled. Look closer and consider how the client learned *not* to feel what they feel. When and how did feeling become not okay?

By seeing the client through the attachment lens, and understanding what is happening or presenting itself to us in session, it's easier to stay empathetic. Why do we need to stay empathetic? Because the therapeutic alliance demands it. Because the human coming to you for help, court-ordered or voluntarily, longs for connection with someone who isn't seeing them as the "bad guy"; they already anticipate judgment. Judgment is a form of condemnation, and there is no way people can change if they feel they're in that type of emotional environment.

If they feel like the therapist is open to really seeing them, they're more likely to open up, allowing them to receive what you're offering. So, the first line of connection, of intervention, in any relationship has to be empathy. And not just occasional empathy when it's easy to understand; but *relentless empathy* in the places that may seem hard to connect with and come alongside of.

Relentless empathy and some uncomfortable truths

As therapists, the first building block of counseling and psychotherapy is an alliance with our client. The therapeutic alliance is the relationship we build with our clients, and it is a sacred one. We are asking clients to step into our office and allow us into their world. We are asking them to expose their hearts, reveal their ugly parts, talk openly about their destructive behaviors, and share vulnerable information that they don't share with most other humans in their lifetime.

We have to have a positive relationship with the client in order for change to be possible. And we know from the *Common Factors*[5] theory and research that the alliance a therapist builds with their client is an essential element for successful therapeutic work to take place. Working with couples means building an alliance with two people in the room and being able to come alongside both people, helping them both to feel fully understood, validated, and empathized with. This is double the emotional work for the therapist because we have to build a connection with two people as opposed to one, which can require more energy.

Building a strong therapeutic alliance with couples can feel especially challenging for therapists. Sometimes one partner comes in completely open and vulnerable and ready for change while the other is dug in, "resistant," and blameful. But we can't just build an alliance with the spouse or partner who is being hurt or abused. It's easier to empathize with the partner that is less in the wrong, more open to change, less angry, and more open to taking responsibility for their part in their disconnection. However, in order for change to happen, we have to empathize with both people in the relationship. We have to hold two different truths in the same emotional space, and help the couple build a secure connection.

Some therapists can fall into the trap of being able to empathize with one partner and get caught pathologizing or judging the other. They stop at the other partner's hurtful behavior and don't lean in to see the human who's longing to be understood in their place of distress and emotional pain but can't put it into words. Sometimes this also happens not only within couples but with an individual client who walks in and conveys no remorse for hurtful words or behavior, and seems set on continuing in their ways. It can be really hard to empathize with someone who doesn't see hurting others as a problem. The path toward empathy can be found when you lean in and help the client expand their emotional window of tolerance, so they can take in the emotional pain they cause others. Many therapists find it difficult to lean in here. Their own defenses might get triggered,[4] and they may lean away from the emotions or the lack thereof, and they can get caught seeing the client as difficult and may look for options of referring the client elsewhere.

Abuse of any kind is not condoned. Empathy is also not a bypass of responsibility for one's abusive behavior. But as a reminder, if we cannot get underneath the abusive behavior to the root, we cannot help it change. We are not condoning abuse; the goal is to help an abuser find more healthy ways of communicating and relating to others. If we get caught up in judgment, it's hard to create an emotionally safe environment for the abuser to confront what's driving the behavior. Remember, underneath all behavior is a person longing to be heard, understood, and loved. The object is to bypass judgment and reach the person underneath. When these types of clients come in for therapy, our job is to help them, not judge them. Most of the time, the relational distress, and sometimes even the physical or legal consequences have already pointed out how ineffective their behavior is. Clients don't need a heaping dose of shame by their therapist on top of it. Shame is a roadblock to people truly seeing their own behavior.

For me, as a therapist, there's nothing worse than hearing other clinicians turn away a difficult client, with the mentality, "I can't help you." Rarely have I encountered clients who can't be helped, or that need a level of care outside of my skillset. As therapists, we're humans with a loving heart and a working brain; yes, we *can* help them. When we turn them away, what we're really saying is, "I see you as beyond help" or "I don't see you as capable of change." This is not a lack skill stance; it's a heart stance, and it says, "I'm shutting my heart off to you, because you're doing 'bad things,' and I'm not willing to be pushed or stretched beyond my comfort zone to help you."

Yes, sometimes there is just cause to use the ethical guidelines that state if someone's needs are beyond our skillset, we are duty-bound to refer them to a higher level of care. In my growing experience as a supervisor of other therapists, I am finding more occurrences where clinicians will hide behind this ethical guideline because they just don't want to work with clients that push them that hard. They aren't willing to push past the limits of their comfort zone to grow and create a new, more highly advanced level of comfort that allows them to sit with even the most challenging of clients. They haven't learned how to have relentless empathy for challenging and difficult clients.

Relentless empathy is a term we use in Emotionally Focused Therapy to describe unceasing empathy for one another.[2] Some of the earliest conceptualizations of this, according to my research, came from Carl Rogers. You may be familiar with the term *unconditional positive regard*. This concept laid the foundation for what we today call *relentless empathy*. Remember, to have empathy means to allow ourselves to access and resonate with, internally, the part of us that is familiar with the feeling being experienced by another. It means to allow ourselves to feel what another person is feeling. Relentless means unceasing, never ending. To have relentless empathy means we never stop having empathy for our client, no matter how challenging or difficult they may seem.

When we have empathy, it is easier to come alongside our clients and have a genuine understanding of their emotional and human experience in a way that the client feels emotionally safe and understood. This is the core of building a positive alliance with a client.

That is one reason why our alliance and ability to have empathy for our clients is so important. Relentless empathy is a sacred duty of the therapist to their clients. We want to teach our clients how to build healthy and secure bonds in their lives outside of the therapy room. But for the short time we see them each week, we are modeling secure attachment and emotional safety. When our clients feel our emotional presence through relentless empathy, it allows them to drop their defenses and emotional swords, and take in new information.

Blocks to empathy: Countertransference

One of the most common blocks that therapists tell me about is countertransference. This is beyond accessing the part of us that is familiar with the emotional experience of the client. It is where the client's behavior triggers or activates feelings in the therapist that then gets directed toward the client. It could be a client who shares the same name as a person you went on a bad date with once. It could be someone that says similar things as a bully from your childhood that makes it hard to relate to the client. However, this isn't limited to negative feelings. This could be having a client who looks and talks like your favorite aunt who passed away, and whenever this client comes into your office, it brings back wonderful memories of your childhood that don't really belong to that client.

When therapists speak of countertransference, they are usually referring to difficult and painful emotions that get triggered and awakened inside of them during the therapy session.[4] Or the client may have a history of behavior that violates a therapist's core beliefs. One of the most common examples I hear is therapists speaking of refusing to see clients who have committed violent crimes. But if every therapist felt this way, what chance or hope would this type of client have for receiving the help needed in order to heal and change their behavior?

Just to clarify, empathy does not mean that we validate hurtful or abusive behavior. We are offering an emotional understanding of the vulnerability and emotions *driving* the hurtful behavior, but not the behavior itself. There is a difference. We all have a choice of how we behave when we feel a certain way. *We can still have relentless empathy without condoning their behavior.* In fact, relentless empathy can create a safe emotional space to confront the hurtful behavior, while also unpacking the emotions and attachment needs underneath it.

Remember that attachment theory accounts for human behavior. Adults, like children, can act out (albeit in very different ways) when they are not feeling loved. Relentless empathy means being able to see underneath the destructive behavior, remembering that there's a deeper reason why it's happening, and being able to see the human underneath who is in pain. Being the therapist of someone guilty of criminal behavior, even serious crimes, gives me a unique opportunity to trace the roots of their behavior to the human underneath who probably never felt loved. It allows me to be with that person in a way that probably no one else has. I use the example of violent crimes because these are usually some of the highest hurdles for therapists to overcome.

When I start looking at the humanness underneath unhealthy behavior, I can find a context through which empathy can flow. I know that not all criminals are remorseful for their behavior. But I also know my best chance to help someone is if I find a way to empathize with them. Humans have the ability to do hurtful things when they are hurting. In my experience, most of the time, they just need someone to show up for them emotionally and understand them by seeing the hurting human underneath. When people feel judged and pathologized, they believe that no one is with them, no one sees them, understands them, and thereby no one is able to truly help them. Many people desperately need to be seen for the human they long to be, or that they really are, even though they might have done something very hurtful or wrong. When people feel seen and understood, they no longer have to fight for this by acting out with destructive behavior.

When I was a student intern, I worked in an outpatient substance abuse agency in lower Manhattan, New York. The majority of clients that came to the agency were ethnic minorities who lived in the projects and were court-ordered for mandatory treatment to help them regulate drug or alcohol use. Many of them had criminal histories and some of them had committed serious crimes such as murder, and had served prison time for it. These clients had initially expressed that they saw me as nothing more than a privileged "Pollyanna" type, incapable of understanding their situation.

I'm happy to say that some of my clients were quite surprised at my ability to empathize with them. One of my most memorable clients had served time for committing murder while running with a street gang. When s/he first started treatment, this person's attitude was very much of a "gang life is the only thing I'm capable of; I'm not interested in changing that" type of mentality. Because s/he had a major crime on their criminal record, despite being incredibly intelligent and gifted at the culinary arts, this client believed no one would be able to see him/her as anything more than just a murderous thug. Even though I had just begun my EFT training, it enabled me to see more.

This particular client has taught me a lot about gang life and how it offered a sense of belonging and community and acceptance in a way that wasn't being offered elsewhere. While I certainly wouldn't condone gang behavior, I could certainly empathize with feeling attached to people that made you feel accepted and valued. I could also empathize with making choices that have life-altering effects, and wandering through life saddled with the consequences, feeling like no one would ever see you as anything else.

As I began relating to the client through this window of empathy, slowly over our sessions, s/he began expressing a desire to leave gang life and find a job doing something they loved: cooking. As I used empathy to stoke these desires, the client also eventually began to see themselves as being able to transform their life and make something better out of it. S/he began to have hope and see themselves as capable. By the end of our treatment, I was helping the client build their resume and apply for culinary school. I don't know what ended up happening to this client, but on our last day meeting together, s/he thanked me for helping them to believe they were actually deserving of a second chance.

Relentless empathy builds safety and alliance that can allow clients to give us the keys to their emotional kingdom. Attachment science and EFT offers us a way to be free of focusing on people's behavior instead of the person. The distress or consequences of someone's words or actions are already present and speak on their own as to their destructive nature in the client's life or relationships with others. We don't need to get wrapped up in judgment or condemnation of the client's behaviors because their distress already does that. Attachment and EFT allow us to start seeing that there is a human being underneath their behavior, and something happened to that human. Our goal as therapists is to find out what that was and piece it all together. But we can't do that without relentless empathy.

Perhaps the best way to have empathy for challenging clients is to remember that we, too, have done things that we regret. We, too, have participated in hurtful behavior that hasn't always been an accurate reflection of our character. When clients tell me they've done hurtful or bad things, I channel this part of my own experience—the part of me that would want to be forgiven and that would want someone to extend the hand of grace and give me a second chance. Having empathy opens the door for second chances for others.

To be empathic: The sponge vs. the mirror

Another block to empathy is being emotionally drained. Many therapists describe themselves as "empaths." What they mean by this is simply that they have a proclivity to feel the emotions of those around them. Being able to feel the emotions of others does not necessarily mean someone is showing empathy, however. I realize this might sound like a strange play on words, but the difference is actually in how the felt emotions are harnessed and expressed in service of the connection with others.

What I find is happening with many "empaths" is that they soak up and absorb the emotions of others, hanging onto the emotions as if they are their own, like an emotional sponge. Though it comes from a caring place, they absorb the emotions of others as if it's their responsibility to fix them. This will quickly weigh you down and drain you. This is why many self-proclaimed "empaths" will keep it low key at social events or avoid large gatherings. It's just too much emotional work for them to be around others. And no wonder! In therapy, being a sponge hijacks your ability to be emotionally present and lowers your ability to be fully empathetic with the person in front of you. As therapists, our job is not to fix people, but rather to facilitate a secure emotional environment and the acquisition of new skills and tools to empower people with the ability to fix themselves.

If you're exhausted and drained, your ability to have empathy will plummet.

When sponging, the emotion becomes about the empath and not the person they're trying to help. I believe this is where being an empath can cross an emotional boundary and is no longer in service of others. Authentic empathy is about others and not self. This can become a negative form of countertransference, hindering the flow of empathy in the therapeutic relationship. Empathy is an emotional muscle memory, an emotional familiarity that allows us to be with the other person on a deeper level in a way that is in service of the other person. As a therapist, all that we do must be in the service of our clients. It's hard to be our best and do what's in service of them if we're emotionally drained.

What many empaths don't realize is that we have the ability to set boundaries when taking in the emotions of those around us. Boundaries with empathy does not mean that we stop having empathy for those around us, nor does it mean that we stop ourselves from feeling the emotions of those around us. What it means is that we can harness the emotions of those around us in a way that doesn't leave us feeling drained. Since emotions compel movement, we can work with the emotion to help move the client in a way that results in more relational success.

Another way to have empathy and come alongside the emotional experience of another person without feeling drained and weighed down is to resonate with another person, as in an emotional echo chamber. We allow their emotions to resonate through us, but in a way that it reflects back toward the other person. Think of it as light bouncing off a mirror, except that the mirror is an emotional process in this case. When light reflects off a mirror, it actually changes direction. So if we allow emotions to reflect through us, they change direction and shift back toward the client; that's when we have true empathy without absorbing the emotions and feeling weighed down. Other people's emotional experiences, no matter how much I relate to them, aren't about me. So when I learned to think of myself as an emotional mirror, as a reflector of light and love, I learned how to reflect back empathy to my clients in a way that didn't weigh me down.

Neurological science actually backs up this mirror method of empathy. Empathy is made possible by the mirror neurons in our brain.[6,7] When these neurons are activated, we mirror back the emotions that we are taking in. Mirror neurons are a cornerstone of empathy,[6] which has important implications for using empathy to build connection with others. Empathy, in that regard, is the ability to mirror back a similar emotional sense that we are experiencing with someone else. How does this mirror of empathy get communicated to our clients? Research says vocal prosody (variations in tone/inflection/rhythm) is the only unambiguous cue of safety,[7,8] because our voices are directly connected to our heart and lungs. Therefore, when we are having empathy for our clients, it will reflect through the prosody in our voice.[8] If you think you can fake empathy, the tone of your voice will give you away.

In multiple ways, the mirror method of empathy more closely follows the point of true empathy and keeps people from feeling depleted or drained. Empathy, after all, is about being with the client; it is not about ourselves, though we may be accessing and touching a deeper part of ourselves in order to more fully connect with others.

Final thoughts on empathy

The good news is that empathy is a renewable source. If we tune in to our own window of tolerance for working with emotions and keep our mental and emotional energy in balance through healthy self-care, we will be able to renew our empathy so that we can continue to become a resource for clients. Our ability to maintain a stance of relentless empathy is vital to shaping therapeutic relationships; to shaping all relationships, and to building the safety required for core, lasting, and effective change to happen.

Questions to consider

1. Reflect on your understanding of sympathy and empathy. What is your own personal definition of empathy?
2. Think of some of your most challenging or difficult clients (past, present, or future). What obstacles have prevented you from having empathy for them?
3. How can you maintain relentless empathy for them going forward?
4. What strategies can you use from this chapter to have empathy for others without draining your emotional resources?

Notes

1 Brown, B. (2013). Brené Brown on Empathy. www.youtube.com/watch?v=1Evwgu369Jw
2 Johnson, S. M. (2019). *Attachment theory in practice: Emotionally focused therapy with individuals, couples and families.* New York, NY: The Guilford Press.
3 Kohut on Empathy. MacIsaac, D. S. (1997). Empathy: Heinz Kohut's contribution. In A. C. Bohart & L. S. Greenberg (Eds.), *Empathy reconsidered: New directions in psychotherapy* (pp. 245–264). Washington, DC: American Psychological Association.
4 On Countertransference in therapy. Valerio, P. (2017). *Introduction To countertransference in therapeutic practice: A Myriad of mirrors.* London: Routledge.
5 On Common Factors in Psychotherapy. Wampold, B. E. (2015). How important are the common factors in psychotherapy? An update. *World Psychiatry: Official Journal of the World Psychiatric Association (WPA), 14*(3): 270–277.
6 The importance of Mirror Neurons. Lamm, C. & Majdandzic, J. (2015). The role of shared neural activations, mirror neurons, and morality in empathy – A critical comment. *Journal of Neuroscience Research, 90*: 15–24.
7 Siegel, D. (2010). *The mindful therapist: A clinician's guide to mindsight and neural integration* (Norton Series on Interpersonal Neurobiology).
8 Porges S. W. (2007). The polyvagal perspective. *Biological Psychology, 74*(2): 116–143.

Chapter 3

Relentless empathy for resistant clients

> Love has an immense ability to help heal the devastating wounds that life sometimes deals us.
> Dr. Susan Johnson, *Hold Me Tight: Your Guide to the Most Successful Approach to Building Loving Relationships*[1]

The sentiment quoted above speaks to one of the most freeing concepts I learned throughout my EFT training: that resistance in therapy can be realized as a client's blocks to doing what we're trying to help them to do.[2] We're trying to help them heal and change and they're digging in, holding back, not moving, and not changing. When therapists come up against a person's blocks, they can get frustrated and some may fall into a frame of thinking that pathologizes or judges the client as difficult and unwilling to change because of this block; because they don't truly understand the block or the function of the block in that moment. It can be challenging for some therapists to maintain their frame of empathy when they encounter clients' blocks even though it is in these moments that empathy is needed most. Without relentless empathy in these moments, it can be challenging to get curious and explore the block, and find a way to work through the block.

In therapy, a block can arise within a person for a variety of reasons. But primarily this block is about something getting triggered inside of the client, something usually painful and vulnerable, scary, or risky, that they're not ready for. Maybe what we're asking them to do is too big, too risky for them to do at this moment. Maybe it brings up something very painful that the client doesn't know how to work through in order to remove the block. Maybe it brings up something inside of the therapist that becomes a trigger for a negative response and the therapist loses their ability to maintain the lens of relentless empathy.

Therapist resistance as a block to relentless empathy

One problem with resistance in clients is not actually the resistance in clients ... it's the resistance in the therapist.[3,4] Just as clients are impacted by pain and negative events from the past, so are therapists. When blocks come up, therapists seem to think of it in a couple of ways. They might see it as they, the therapist, is doing something wrong, like it's a sign that they're not good enough as a therapist to get the client to do what they want them to do. Or, they see it as something's wrong with the client. This is where therapists might get tempted to start using some type of pathological label for the client. When clients get resistant in session, it can cause therapists to lose their footing and get off track. When this happens, they can fall out of the window of empathy. Meaning, they stop seeing the client's reactive behavior as an ineffective plea for help, attention, care, acceptance, etc. and we start judging them. Self of the therapist issues (what happens inside of the therapist) can be a block to having relentless empathy and being therapeutically effective in our work.

If therapists have unresolved wounds from their past, family of origin issues, unprocessed trauma, personal biases, or struggle with their own self-esteem, they are more likely to lose their balance in the therapy room.[3] When therapists are balanced and emotionally healthy, they are able to embody congruence and empathy. Congruence, or therapists walking their talk, is an important quality for therapists to have, and is also listed as a therapist quality under professional ethical standards for the counseling professions.[5,6,7,8] Therapists are strongly urged to do their own therapeutic work starting from their entry into a graduate school counseling program. However, if therapist's have not resolved their issues, or are in denial of the negative impact certain events are having, they will be more likely to have a variety of reactions and get triggered in session by certain client reactivity or situations. This might include getting stuck, avoiding certain issues or dismissing the significance of certain issues for the client, avoiding going deeper into live emotions, or losing focus.

Of course it's not possible to be congruent and balanced 100% of the time. But if we're avoidant or resistant to looking at our own blocks to empathy and fully leaning into clients' struggles and emotions, even if we don't understand or we don't agree, then we are doing a disservice to ourselves and our clients. However, the more we are aware of our own blocks and triggers, and the more willing we are to examine what comes up for us, and work through it, the more easily we will get our balance back and resume our focus, empathy, and therapeutic effectiveness.

Many therapists were taught how to view their clients' distress and how to intervene from a place of emotional distance, but we haven't really been trained on how to use ourselves as an instrument in the process. We as therapists are the best part of the therapeutic process if we're willing to use ourselves as an instrument of connection to help clients.[9] This process requires us to be emotionally balanced ourselves,[10] and to build a solid connection with the client (therapeutic alliance), which we can't do without being able to have relentless empathy for our clients.[2]

When clients come in that are challenging or difficult, or dig in and are resistant, how do we show up for them in our sessions? Many therapists dig in to their own positions, and try to coach the client around their block, or they pathologize them: "Great! you're a narcissist." That means go see a psychiatrist, take some medication, read a book, or in other words, "you're a human being with this nice ugly label and I see you as beyond hope of changing." That's not a client block. That's a *therapist* block. Self of the therapist issues can become a major barrier to having relentless empathy and building a strong therapeutic alliance.[3] And if we can't build that strong therapeutic alliance, can you imagine being able to do any kind of effective work with that client? If we can lean into our own blocks, and work on them outside of session, we're more likely to be able to quickly regain our focus,[10] and resume our ability to have relentless empathy for the client.

> Presence, attunement and resonance within our self will lead to greater presence, attunement and resonance with our clients.[10]

Client blocks in therapy

It takes a lot of courage to sit with another human being and really lean into their struggles. And without the lens of relentless empathy, leaning into our clients' struggles is going to be really challenging. The clients are not trying to be difficult on purpose. Many of them don't know how to trust others with their deepest parts of self or how to make sense of their painful experiences. Resistance popping up in therapy is actually a good sign. It means their system is being destabilized, and when we're trying to interrupt patterns of unhealthy strategies, we need the negative patterns to destabilize.

There's a redemptive part of struggle and pain. There are good reasons why clients feel the way they do and behave the way they do. It may not necessarily be effective or healthy, but we can't help clients create that second order change without being able to validate, understand, and go underneath the good reasons they have for doing what they do, even though the behaviors are no longer beneficial. Honestly, it wasn't until I figured out that most people are humans who have good reasons for doing what they do that I was able to really empathize with even the most difficult and resistant clients.

Attachment science tells us that the behaviors associated with how clients deal with their distress is about regulating emotion. Behavior is simply the tangible display of how people regulate (or dysregulate) their emotions. If the client you're working with cannot regulate their emotions, whose help do you think they need? They need us, their therapist. If we can't maintain the lens of relentless empathy, we won't be able to lean into client resistance and remove the blocks. A lack of empathy can become a therapist block to doing effective therapeutic work.

As therapists, we are responsible for the process not the outcome. All we can do is open up space and try to choreograph new moves for the clients to change. But really it's the work, the vulnerability and emotional risks the clients have to take, that will determine the outcome.

Research shows we as humans do better coping with distress by connecting with others than we do alone.[2,11] That's not just a guess or a hope. It's a fact. And our job as therapists is about building a safe place, a safe therapeutic connection to create some space in the therapy room for clients to be able to work through their blocks. Relentless empathy is what helps us *shape* our therapeutic alliance,[2] by creating connection and building emotional safety to do some of their most courageous, vulnerable work.

Overcoming resistance in therapy

Having relentless empathy helps us to be able to go under the surface of resistance and be able to organize and make sense of what's happening. Why do people defend themselves the way they do in the moment of distress? Someone looks away, someone gets angry, someone goes silent, someone gets reactive, or someone gives up. This isn't the client choosing to be difficult because of some pathology. These are all triggers and indicators of live emotions and we have to be able to recognize this and work with it in the moment that it's happening. But when we go into our heads and start pathologizing, labeling, and judging, what happens to the client in that moment? They get left alone and abandoned in their moment of distress when they need us the most. In these moments, the client needs us to show up for them, see them in their distress, and show them that it matters.

We also have to be able to start harnessing these emotions so we can work with the blocks (resistance). When clients get resistant, we need to be able to lean in, explore, and get specific about their dilemma, get really clear. It's leaning in and unpacking the blocks that lets clients have much more access to having new conversations and change. Many therapists try to rush their clients into change when they don't quite have all the pieces in place for the new moves to really take root.

To gather all of the pieces and get them into place, we have to be able to lean in, in their stance of resistance. It's that relentless empathy stance that allows you to lean in with curiosity to unpack the block. When you as the therapist don't know why, despite your brilliant efforts and interventions, your client isn't changing, or is still defending their position, if you trust the process of emotion, the client's resistance will become clearer. Their resistance, their block, is saying something is happening in that person that is not ready for your brilliant interventions. Get curious about it. If you get curious about it, you'll be working with what is actually happening live in the moment, and being present and engaged with it. That's when we as therapists will be doing some of our most effective work.

Unfortunately, most of us are either out in front of our clients' blocks, too far ahead of the blocks trying to get clients to move ahead too fast, or we're falling behind their blocks. In either direction, this is where therapists might start trying to coach their clients, trying to get them to where we want them to be. In this process we end up leaving the present moment and what is actually happening. Of course it seems easier to just turn to your clients in couple's therapy and say to one partner, "if you would just be softer and nicer, your partner probably wouldn't shut down and go away"; And to the other partner, "if you wouldn't go away, because you know it does bad things to your partner, they would feel a lot safer too. And things would be a lot different." Sounds like we're doing really good work doesn't it? The clients are agreeing, they're nodding, so we're done right? Unfortunately, the moment they get back into that triggered place, or that emotion comes alive for them again at home, and we're wanting them to do something different without having them try it out in therapy first, they're going to get the same blocks and the problem is going to repeat itself.

Many therapists when clients get resistant and a block presents itself will try to push the client into change. "Oh you don't want to do this? Well let me explain all of the good reasons why you should do this." What is that going to do with the resistance? We can't coach a client around their blocks and resistance; it simply isn't effective enough to produce lasting second order change. And if most of the time our strategy is to go around resistance and blocks, where are we leaving our clients? Alone to deal with these blocks, without our help outside of therapy. This is not such a safe way to deal with their blocks, especially because much of the time, clients don't even know their own blocks or how to make sense of them. Clients may say, "I don't know why I'm not able to tell my spouse the truth, something just happens that stops that process." If the therapist isn't going to get curious and go deeper, and instead tries to coach the client around their block, then all that's going to happen is the block is going to stay outside of their awareness, lurking in the dark waiting to come up again. And it's probably going to come up again at home.

If we could just explain what needs to happen to clients, especially when they get blocked and triggered, then clients would never really need to actually come to therapy and could just as easily create change from self-help books and friendly advice! But we already know that just offering explanations isn't enough to trump our emotional experience. This is why leaning into their live emotional experiences with curiosity and relentless empathy is so important for experientially working with client blocks and creating change.

Working with emotion can be really challenging for therapists, especially if they themselves aren't even comfortable with emotion. So many therapists try to play it safe by working at an emotional distance where they're most comfortable and feel the most safe themselves. It's a lot easier for a therapist to try to work with emotional blocks cognitively than to lean in and have the client go experientially into their live emotional process. But when we do that we miss the magic of creating behavior change. Clients actually have to experientially learn how to put words to their emotional experience, and share it with others as a clear emotional signal.

We cannot help clients move around resistance and remove blocks if we are judging and pathologizing them. The path to change starts with connection first. The therapeutic connection is strongest when it's founded on relentless empathy. If you don't have empathy, you don't have connection, you don't have emotionally safety, and you don't have a path toward successfully creating change. If you don't have that lens of relentless empathy, and you try to jump in and coach a resistant client around a block by giving advice, your feedback will sound like criticism. Who wants to pay someone to criticize them? Most clients get enough of that at home and in their relationships. We have to be validating and affirming of the clients, not just the ones that are easy to relate to, but all of them. The challenging, difficult, and resistant ones too!

Maintaining relentless empathy

It can be difficult to lean into highly reactive and hurtful clients. It can trigger something that's familiar inside of the therapist that makes it hard to want to go deeper underneath that behavior. Maybe there's something about the coldness of that client that feels really familiar to our heart and we get a trigger. Or maybe there's something about the way the client yells that makes it hard to stay present with them. But if we can't get comfortable with reactivity and working with emotion, then when these blocks come up in therapy, we will never be able to work with them. Being able to identify our own triggers and blocks[10] to having relentless empathy will help us be able to change our stance and keep our focus on going where we need to go with the client. If we become really aware of what triggers us and gets in the way and blocks our empathy, then we can change it and be able to set it aside and go back to keeping our focus.

Relentless empathy is the foundation upon which therapists will build a strong and safe therapeutic alliance.[2] Viewing client's distress through the attachment framework will have a huge impact on how you make meaning of your client's behavior, and will shape the interventions you do with them and why. It will also help you, the therapist, to better maintain a stance of relentless empathy. Therapists need to have a good conceptual game plan of where they're going in the moment based on relentless empathy. If you don't have that strong therapeutic alliance built, and you're trying to get your client to open up, they're going to get blocked!

The best thing we as therapists can do is learn to trust the process of emotions. It may be messy, but it is a predictable process, and there is powerful information contained in these emotional signals that we receive from our clients. Their blocks are emotional signals indicating there's a problem, something feels scary, something doesn't feel good, or they're unsure if it's safe to trust. When we can expect blocks and get comfortable working with live emotion in the room, it will be easier for therapists to lean into blocks and work with them as they come up. Notice the blocks that come up and be prepared to stay with them and work with the blocks rather than attempt to maneuver around them. If there are any self of the therapist countertransference issues that are getting triggered and blocking your ability to have relentless empathy for your clients, become as aware as you can of these blocks and triggers. Seek the guidance of a supervisor or professional mentor, and if necessary, work through deeper personal blocks with your own therapist. Exploring self of the therapist is an invaluable experience that will reap rewards for the client, the therapeutic relationship, and the therapist.

Questions to consider

1. How comfortable am I working with emotion?
2. How do I feel about feeling?
3. If not, what blocks or gets in the way of my ability to tolerate emotional experiencing?
4. Have I fully resolved any past hurts or traumas with attachment figures?
5. Are there still certain types of clients or issues I'm uncomfortable working with?
6. If yes, have you sought supervision around these issues?
7. When you get triggered in session, what do you do? Do you go into your head? Do you pull back emotionally?
8. Whatever move you make when triggered, how does this impact the client?
9. How does this move impact the therapy session?
10. How does this move impact your overall work?

Notes

1 Johnson, S. M. (2008). *Hold me tight: Seven conversations for a lifetime of love*. New York, NY: Little, Brown and Company.
2 Johnson, S. M. (2019). *Attachment theory in practice: Emotionally focused therapy with individuals, couples and families*. New York, NY: The Guilford Press.
3 On Countertransference in therapy. Valerio, P. (2017). *Introduction to countertransference in therapeutic practice: A myriad of mirrors*. London: Routledge.
4 Newman, C. F. (2002). A cognitive perspective on resistance in psychotherapy. *Journal of Clinical Psychology, 58*: 165–174.
5 Counseling Codes of Ethics. American Counseling Association. (2014). *ACA code of ethics*. Alexandria, VA: American Counseling Association.
6 Counseling Codes of Ethics. American Psychological Association. (2002). Ethical principles of psychologists and code of conduct. *American Psychologist, 57*(12): 1060–1073.
7 Counseling Codes of Ethics. American Association of Marriage and Family Therapy. (2015). *AAMFT code of ethics*. Alexandria, VA: American Association for Marriage and Family Therapists.
8 Counseling Codes of Ethics. NASW Code of Ethics (Guide to the Everyday Professional Conduct of Social Workers). Washington, DC: NASW, 2008.
9 Use of self of the therapists in psychotherapy. Siegel, D. J. (2010). *The mindful therapist: A new approach to cultivating your own neural integration from the inside out*. Eau Claire, WI: CMI/Premier Education Solutions.

10 Siegel, D. (2010). *The mindful therapist: A clinician' guide to mindsight and neural integration* (Norton Series on Interpersonal Neurobiology). New York, NY: W. W. Norton & Company.
11 Coan, J. A., & Maresh, E. L. (2014). Social baseline theory and the social regulation of emotion. In J. J. Gross (Ed.), *Handbook of emotion regulation* (pp. 221–236). New York, NY: The Guilford Press.

Chapter 4

Relentless empathy for personality disordered clients

> Rarely can a response make something better. What makes something better is connection.
>
> Brené Brown in *Daring Greatly*

When I hear clinicians use the words "personality disorder," I cringe. I would like to say that most of the time when I hear it, it's used in its proper clinical diagnostic context, but unfortunately, it's usually in a way that is a misuse of the term. These terms have even become misused outside of psychology, becoming labels haphazardly thrown around as a socially constructed weapon, which makes them really dangerous. The use of these terms has gotten used more regularly by people who are of course not clinically trained, which diminishes the value and utility of the word clinically. What used to be an actual clinical diagnostic term to help the profession treat a problem has gotten twisted into something that is misused as a label of judgment. And I'm sorry to hear other clinicians participate in this misuse all the time.

I often come across pop psychology articles written by other therapists throwing around this term. What they're really doing is applying a label that lacks empathy and is highly reactive and focuses on their own self-interests. With the way it's used today, this term could describe half of the world's population and I'm sure they're not all truly personality disordered. I've even had clients tell me that their previous therapist told them they were in a relationship with a personality disordered person, and that they should think about getting out of the relationship. Not only is this highly unethical, but it was not what the client wanted.

While some people do express relief to be given an official diagnosis, feeling like there's some clarity to what's happening with them, others feel deeply pathologized or turned off because their partner is being pathologized. When I sat and thought about some of these terms, like "borderline personality disorder," for example, I wondered, what are they on the border of? Are they on the border between having a personality or having no personality? The border between having a disorder and being normal? The border of becoming serial killers? What on earth is this "border" they speak of? (It turns out that originally it meant on the border between psychosis (not treatable) and neurosis (treatable).[1])

I feel like this term has become a judgment of character. I also think that if it were applied to me, it would feel like someone was tallying up my behavior and evaluating it as a character defect rather than something legitimate that was actually happening to me. This is especially true if this person is a therapist—the person I'm paying to help and understand me (not to just tell me that I'm a defective person).

In my experience, when therapists use the term "personality disorder," they are describing a client who they feel is difficult. They may not realize how judgmental they sound, as they spew the words "borderliner" or "narcissist." These two types of clients have a good reason for what's happening in their world, and deserve the same empathy, attention, and respect as non-difficult clients.

When we start throwing around labels, it's like we're saying, "you are sick," "you are not capable of change," or "you are beyond hope" instead of seeing personality disorders for what they really are: a result of extreme insecure attachment and usually trauma as well. The additional danger of this is when clients see themselves as sick, they won't tend to take responsibility for their behavior and pass it off as "this is happening because I'm sick," but not as behavior they can exert some control over to change. Additionally, they end up going to their general medical doctors or psychiatrists for pills because they're "sick" and don't believe therapy is the needed remedy for change.

The way these types of clients tend to behave in therapy is very reactive. Clinicians get caught up in the reactive behavior in front of them, often becoming triggered by it, and they stop seeing the reactive behavior for what it really is: a coping strategy. We start compiling a list of symptoms and we stop there, without looking for something deeper.

When judgment starts, empathy ends.

Brené Brown, one of the greatest modern contributors to research on empathy today, really nailed it in her quote at the opening of this chapter. Responses without empathy really aren't effective in making things better. It is connection that makes things better and empathy is our vehicle for connection, especially with a person whom we find challenging, resistant, or downright difficult.

If attachment teaches us anything, it's that there is always a reason why people do what they do, and there are very legitimate emotions driving whatever it is they are doing. I'm not suggesting that what they are doing is healthy or functional. But if I don't look for what's driving it and I don't help heal the person, the only thing I've provided is a band-aid solution.

Most therapists would describe narcissism and borderline personality disorders as the two most common and challenging types of personality disorders they work with. I believe it's because both types of disorders come with a lot of reactive behavior that tends to push people away, and most people don't understand the behavior. That's because they don't truly understand attachment. This is why I keep stressing attachment; it helps us understand behavior, and understanding behavior helps us stay in a frame of relentless empathy. This is the most effective way for the client to receive the best care and help they need and deserve.

I once heard a colleague say that the behaviors of personality disordered clients make them really hard to love, while thinking about referring the client to another therapist because they didn't want to work that hard. My heart sank. I understand that some people don't make it easy to get close to them and love them. But isn't that what we're here for? To help them? If we all took this same stance, we would be perpetuating the same messages of abandonment and rejection they've, more than likely, already been receiving for part or most of their life.

This is where relentless empathy becomes so crucial. If we can see these particular types of clients through the attachment lens, and recognize their behavior is a strategy rooted in insecure attachment, then we can recognize that they are doing the best they can to feel loved and worthwhile. It's hard *not* to have empathy when you see the person in front of you as desperately wanting to be loved and feel worthy.

The research is clear. The majority of clients with a diagnosable personality disorder have some form of adverse childhood experiences (childhood trauma)[2,3,4,5,6] and parents or caregivers that were emotionally unavailable, abusive, or flat-out neglectful. Many factors can influence the parent-child relationship from infancy.[7] Some children have challenging temperaments and they may have a parent who is emotionally avoidant and closed off as well. The parent and child can clash, and the interactions between them become challenging and negative. When children are emotionally reactive in a negative way, and highly impulsive, they can be challenging to raise, and not all parents are up to the challenge emotionally. Also, if the parents have unresolved trauma or mental illness, even poverty can strain the emotional interactions between the parent and child.[7]

Neglect is insidious for humans.[8] Some children didn't grow up with parents who hit or verbally abused them, but to not have your parent emotionally show up for you, to love you for who you are, can cause children to grow up with a negative view of self. Neglect can also cause children to grow up with a lot of avoidant strategies, and struggle to let people deeply close to them. This starts off their personality development in a negative and insecure way. These beliefs are likely to remain over time unless the person has had positive and secure emotionally corrective attachment experiences. Think about growing up not believing or being sure that you are loved. Later, as an adult in a romantic relationship, it's hard to trust that love because it's contradictory to everything you grew up believing about yourself. The point I'm trying to make is that at the heart of many personality disorders is a lack of trust.

Trauma also plays a major role in personality disorders and in the development of lacking trust toward others.[3] There's a huge overlap between trauma and personality disorders, and clinicians in general agree on this. If only the DSM would catch up and include this in their formal list of diagnostic criteria for personality disorders.

Personality disorders and trauma

Famous addiction specialist Gabor Maté[9] once said in an interview that trauma is not what bad thing happens to you, it's what's happens inside of you as a result of what has happened to you. Remember that secure attachment helps us have psychological resilience when dealing with painful events. When a person experiences trauma and they do not have a secure attachment figure to help them cope, soothe, or organize reality around the events that happened, they are more likely to be traumatically affected and less likely to adjust and recover in a healthy and secure way.

This is also visible in clients who had childhood neglect or parents who were emotionally unavailable.[10] When a person experiences something traumatic, usually in childhood, that unavailability teaches them *not* to go to their parents or someone close to them, and that others won't be available for them. This is where people start to develop a deep self-reliance, for their survival, which is a hallmark of narcissistic personality disorder.[11]

What's worse, as in the case of borderline personality disorder, a form of disorganized attachment, is the damage that occurs when the trauma is committed by an attachment figure.[12] It is hard for the brain to rectify that this family member, or primary caregiver, who's supposed to protect them is now causing them harm. This could be a parent being extremely critical and emotionally abusive to their child, or emotionally bringing the child close and then manipulating them, or sexual abuse. This is where you might also find other disorders like Dissociative Identity Disorder,[6] as the brain tries to cope with and organize conflicting information. The brain may create splits to contain the good parts of the interactions with the attachment figure, while the child is trying to protect himself or herself during these abusive moments.

The attachment figure who abandons or rejects their child during moments of distress or need can be even more insidious. We call this attachment trauma.[7] Attachment trauma can occur in two ways. The first is described above, where an attachment figure is committing traumatic harm or violating physical boundaries.[7] The second is when a traumatic situation occurs and the attachment figure turns away or fails to show up emotionally with empathy, comfort, and support. For example, if a child is being bullied at school and tells their parent(s), and their parents dismiss the significance and tell them to tough it out or work it out on their own.

In the case of disorganized attachment,[6] a staple for borderline personality disorder, the parent(s) can be highly inconsistent with their love and care. One or both parents might be very loving and welcoming in some moments, but suddenly angry, rejecting, dismissive, or critical the next. The triggers for this sudden shift may feel completely random and ambiguous to the child, providing no clear way for him or her to organize or make sense of what's happening. They have no idea how to make sense of what they see in others as well. They distrust affection offered by others because they know it might go away. This can also cause them to be guarded when others try to get close to them. They may start to panic when they sense others pulling away and detaching. Or they may get anxious by the lack of physical proximity, and see it as a danger that the other will never return.

Sometimes there can be double trauma in cases of sexual abuse committed by a family member. When the trauma is reported to the parent or caregiver, the child is accused of making up the story. Not only did they just experience great harm, but both the harm and care are being denied by their attachment figures. This is probably one of the deepest forms of attachment betrayal.

Altogether, neglect and attachment trauma can impact the development of not only the personality, but the development of trust. It would be really hard to trust that others love you if your parents never expressed love for you or showed you that you were loved. Likewise it would be hard to develop trust for others if the experiences you had growing up were with people who were supposed to be protecting you from harm and ended up hurting, abusing, or turning their back on you.

When people, especially children, go through these traumatic experiences, the brain has no idea how to organize this information. It has no idea how to discern who's safe from who's not, what the cues for danger are, or whether people can be trusted when they try to get emotionally close to you.

This often shows up in the therapy room as "black-and-white" thinking or splitting. A lot is written about how maladaptive black-and-white thinking is harmful, but not a lot of attention is given to how these strategies come into effect. If we can't understand them, we can't validate their function for the client as a safety mechanism, and therefore we will come up against the client's guardedness and unwillingness to part with this strategy.

Black-and-white thinking is merely a way of organizing the world in an extremely clear way. There are some things in this world that are black and white. But there is a lot of gray as well, and those with insecure attachment styles have very low tolerance for the gray area, the ambiguity that lies in the unknown. This is why they desperately try to push and pull everything into an all-or-nothing, this-way-or-that-way, black-and-white type of tunnel vision. It is the only way they know how to feel safe and predict what's around the next corner.

The deeper the trauma, the more someone will dig in and hold onto these black-and-white, or defensive, coping strategies.[12] It's not pathological. It's survival. If it's the only way they know how to feel safe in the world, then it's understandable why they feel the need to organize their experiences in this way. When we help clients move closer to secure attachment, they will become more comfortable with the gray area in between. The more securely attached people become, the more confident they become in their resources found in others, and in their own abilities to adapt and meet novel situations appropriately and effectively.[13]

These traumatic experiences often culminate in the development of disorganized attachment,[6] and the reactive coping strategies consistent with this type of insecure attachment coincide with the symptoms of personality disorders.

Blocks to empathy for personality disorders

Without really understanding the root of personality disorders in our pivotal negative human experiences it's easy to misread what's happening and get triggered ourselves when the clients start acting out in session.

I know it might sound strange, but I think we get triggered *because* we feel empathy. The problem is that many people haven't mastered how to work through the pain and emotion that comes alive inside of them so that they can set it aside and still find a path toward empathy for their personality disordered client. I think a lot of people, therapists included, have been in a relationship with someone who was hurtful and maybe even emotionally traumatizing. Maybe we were traumatized ourselves and never connected the dots with how deep those scars run and impact how we perceive or treat others.

Whether it was experiencing a lack of emotional caring by another, or seemingly erratic, messy, and dramatic behavior, most of us know what it feels like to be on the receiving end of such behavior, and that is what gets triggered when these clients are in our therapy room. Our empathy is triggered for the partner on the receiving end of this behavior. For example, I once had a client who I will call "Bill." He was coming to me for couples counseling but was highly reactive in session with his wife, and would almost sort of puff up his chest, stand up and yell, and occasionally storm out of the session when I explored his moves in his negative relationship cycle. It was easy to have empathy for his wife who was on the receiving end of such behavior, but Bill was also in a lot of pain, and that was at the heart of his behavior. I had to recognize that his reactivity was a plea for help to see his pain. Without being able to have relentless empathy for his pain, I would have never been able to calm his reactivity and go underneath his behavioral strategies that were so ineffective in evoking a caring response from his partner. Many times we fail to offer empathy to the one who is highly reactive, and we end up emotionally abandoning them or rejecting them.

When it comes to seeing couples, it can be easier to resonate with the experience of the partner being hurt or dumped on, and we forget to dig into, explore, understand, and find a way to empathize with the one engaging in such behavior. Also, some of these clients tend to get reactive in session and oftentimes make the therapist the target of their emotion. Reactive emotions can be hard to contain in session, especially for a therapist not comfortable with working with emotion. Some of our EFT trainers call reactive emotion a soup of secondary emotion because it's messy and can be all over the place. Of course every therapist wants to do a good job, our ability to continue to bring in new clients depends on it. Hearing a client angrily question our ability to help them, cast blame in our direction, or insult us can feel unnerving.

We, as the therapist, can lose our sense of being grounded and become defensive or inadvertently take sides with one partner over the other. When therapists haven't been trained in this area, they don't understand what's happening in front of them. It's not that they're unqualified or lack talent. The client is simply losing their emotional balance and is looking for a sense of emotional safety with us. They want to know that we get their pain and can help them eliminate it. Their reactivity is part of their attachment strategy, and unless we recognize it it's easier to get hijacked by the triggers and lose our ability to empathize with the client. I call it falling out of the empathy window.

Another reason that clients with personality disorders can be challenging for therapists is that many of them are rigid and stuck in their positions when they come in, and don't seem open to or willing to accept direction. Even when we have empathy, it can still be frustrating because internally it can feel like, "I'm here to help you. I see your pain. Why won't you let me help you?" They can feel very resistant while continuing behavior that we know isn't helping them reach their goals for love and connection and success. Remember, resistance is viewed in EFT as asking a client to do something they're not ready to do, or asking them to bite off a piece that's too big to chew. This behavior is part of their emotional attachment survival system. It may not be helping them, but, in many cases, it's all they know. So asking them to do something different is asking them to take risks, which can feel scary, especially if they don't have a secure attachment figure to help them as they take these risks.

When you can see reactive and resistant behavior for what it is, it is so much easier to stay in the empathy window, validate their experience and fears, and help them take new steps. One thing I like about EFT is we don't want to take away a person's defenses, because we know they'll just dig in and try to hold onto them all that much more. But when we can empathize with their emotional experience and their need to have these defenses, they will eventually get to the place where they see their own defense as an ineffective strategy of getting what they need.[13] We're handing their defenses to them, walking side by side with them emotionally, so that they will put their own defenses down. It's like saying to a client, *"I get why you need that emotional shield and it's okay that you need that shield for now. We'll work on making it safe for you to put your shield down when you're ready."* This, in essence, is exactly what happens with these clients. When we hand them their defenses through empathy and validation, we start creating emotional safety. The more emotionally safe the environment becomes, the less they'll need to keep their defenses up. It also helps empower clients and allows them to heal and grow emotionally. This is especially important for clients who we believe lack empathy or responsibility for their behavior, including their emotional growth, which can be symptomatic of personality disorders.

Narcissistic clients

When I hear other therapists talk about a narcissistic client, they are often describing a client who seems to lack empathy and focuses on serving his or her own needs at the exclusion of others. Additionally, I read so many articles that seem to be painting narcissistic people as the new psychopaths and abusers. I'm not suggesting people stay in an abusive relationship. But even abuse can be confronted, dealt with, and is capable of change in therapy.

Have therapists and the media at large completely lost empathy? Do they truly see narcissists as being incapable of change? *That is what therapy is for.* But this can't be done if therapists are telling clients to get out of relationships with narcissists instead of inviting them into the room for some work. This change is only possible when we can retain empathy for both clients, including the one we may see as narcissistic. While lack of empathy and serving one's own needs may be a symptom of narcissism, they are also symptomatic of many types of emotional and mental health problems, and at the core of these symptoms is insecure attachment.

The term narcissism originated from Greek mythology,[14] specifically the story of Narcissus, who is said to have fallen in love with his own reflection. He drowned pining away for the reflection, and while the Greeks believed vanity was unlucky and this was a story conveying a cultural morè, I wonder how the story might have been told differently had someone examined Narcissus's attachment environment. Further Greek writings on Narcissus said that it was actually more likely that he was in despair over the loss of his twin sister,[15] his exact counterpart, and staring at his reflection was the way in which he was able to remember her features (Encyclopedia Britannica online). So it really is all about attachment, even in Greek mythology!

The way narcissism is currently conceptualized by the DSM-V[16] is: an excessive reliance on others for definition of self and to regulate self-esteem; exaggerated self-value (either negative or positive); goals set on the basis of gaining approval from others; expectations that are either exceptionally high or low (pertaining to a sense of entitlement); impaired ability to show empathy; impairment in intimacy (having superficial relationships to boost one's ego); covert or overt feelings of grandiosity; and/or excessive attempts to seek admiration or attention from others.[16]

In reading over the DSM-V description of narcissism, the symptoms immediately scream out "attachment issues!" I think the very definition of narcissism is contradictory. The term narcissism gets used to describe someone who is so full of self-value that it feels like an affront to others. In society we tend to correlate security with positive self-value, and someone with inflated self-value must feel really solid in who they are. Wrong. Do secure people feel the need to excessively pursue the attention and admiration of others? Do they live or die by the approval of others? No, they don't. But if we stop at the title of narcissism, the name itself, which has become a label eliciting negative feelings on the inside, then we, too, become guilty of a superficial judgment, and empathy stops. But if we are able to recognize narcissism through the attachment lens, we can resume empathy and work on rehabilitating the client's attachment system.

Narcissists are not secure people. By definition, how can you really be full of yourself if you're secure? The very definition demonstrates the façade by which narcissists operate, and we must not be guilty of evaluating people with narcissistic behaviors on that same level. We must go deeper. Therapists find narcissists so challenging mainly because narcissists lack empathy.

However, contrary to pop psychology articles, narcissistic clients do not lack empathy because of some psychopathology. They do not lack empathy because they are bad people. They lack empathy because they have cut off their emotions because they have been hurt, abandoned, and rejected, and only know how to trust and rely on the love and care they can give themselves. It is the only form of safe attachment they can experience, which isn't by nature a real or healthy attachment relationship; it's avoidant attachment. For them, it's "rely on self, love self, let no one else impact you."

One of the main reasons narcissists lack empathy is their proclivity to numb and avoid emotions, especially the emotions of others. In order for someone to feel empathy, they have to be able to feel. They have to allow something from another person to resonate with and touch something within themselves. In order to do this, one has to be in contact with his or her emotions—not just surface-level emotions, but all of their emotions. In order to feel empathy, one has to allow themselves to be impacted by other's emotions. Narcissists do not allow themselves to be impacted by emotions—not their own and thereby not others. The process of empathy cannot take place when they do not allow themselves to feel. When there is emotional cut-off, there can be no empathy.

Think of excessive self-love as a golden parachute filled with such magnitude that the person would never have to touch the ground or, in other words, feel vulnerable. The risk of getting out of one's own way and allowing themselves to come back to earth is feeling what the narcissist tries so hard to avoid: vulnerability. Somewhere along the line, narcissists began emotionally taking care of themselves because no one else was; or at least they perceived no one else was. Believing that no one is there for you can leave people feeling alone, abandoned, rejected, and unloved. While some may employ different strategies to cope with these feelings, narcissists have developed their own strategies. They developed a survival strategy of not letting anyone come close enough to hurt them, to never be the victim because that would hurt too much and they might get taken advantage of. So they stay distant, and because of the distance, they don't attach.

Narcissists have learned that others are not emotionally reliable, that they cannot count on others to be there for them, so they deactivate (turn off) and turn away from their need for others, and learn to survive by taking care of their own needs. This includes emotional needs for praise, adoration, acceptance, and love. We know that survival strategies work because people survive the danger with these strategies. Surviving can reinforce these strategies. However, surviving isn't thriving, and over time, having this become the only survival strategy, one becomes less flexible in emotional situations, and their strategy becomes very narrow. Rigidity in behaviors can be the very emotional survival strategy that kills off the attachment connections, not allowing those bonds to survive.

Psychology divides narcissism into two types: overt and covert. Overt narcissism is more like having a grandiose ego or beliefs of grandeur, aggressive behavior, and extreme demands for attention, while covert narcissism is more like feelings of persecution, anxiety, and hypersensitivity to being criticized (see the DSM-V[16]). The narrow focus of a narcissist is "I can only rely on myself," which leaves no room for others in a narcissist's inner world. The double bind of a narcissist is that there is no success without the approval of others, yet a narcissist will vehemently deny that they have needs and a reliance on the approval of others.

Why? Not because they are terrible, self-absorbed people, though it may look like that on the outside. It's because it is too vulnerable and too risky for them to admit that. This opens them up for rejection. Narcissists are all smoke and mirrors. They'll distract you with their confidence and ego over here so you don't look over there to the real person underneath who is actually vulnerable. In some ways, they are some of the world's greatest illusionists. They like to create an illusion that they have no vulnerabilities, no weaknesses, and no scars. They want you to believe in the golden image of perfection they have painted for you. And some of them do a great job of fooling the people around them, and fooling the general public (think of politicians). But if you can get close enough to a narcissist, you will begin to see beneath the surface. You will see through the façade to the person who is far more insecure than they will ever admit to others because it is not emotionally safe to do so.

In this survival strategy, a narcissist will come to their own rescue by reassuring themselves, offering themselves praise and reassurance, reminding themselves why they're worthy and deserving of love, affection, and praise, while others on the outside may view this as stroking their own ego. But what is the alternative? Feel vulnerable and unsure without the safety and assurance of a secure base to be there for them? Feel imperfect, flawed, unworthy, and all alone in these feelings?

Sometimes asking them to open up or be vulnerable is like asking them to risk without an emotional safety net. Like asking them to jump off a cliff without a parachute, or some assurance that someone is at the bottom to catch them and keep them safe. If they do have a partner who wants to be there, with their history of insecure attachment, a narcissist wouldn't know *how* to trust their partner because they have no idea how to feel safe with their vulnerability in the hands or heart of another. Vulnerability is far too risky of a venture, especially if they come from a background where no one has been there for them or has abandoned or rejected them in a time of vulnerability and need. I have found this to be a common experience among clients I have had or people whom I have met that others would identify as "narcissistic."

On the receiving end of this, partners or close loved ones in relationship with the narcissist may feel pushed away, dismissed, or rejected, and that there is no room for their emotions or opinions. Many who have been in a relationship with a narcissist have been hurt. Their narcissistic partner may get really reactive and angry when they do try to assert their opinions. Narcissistic clients may also present as resistant in therapy, and may reject any intervention that puts some responsibility or accountability for their hurtful behavior in their hands.

I've not met a person yet with self-reported or partner-reported narcissistic qualities who didn't have insecure attachment. If the narcissistic client comes from an attachment frame where they learned others are not available for them to help meet their emotional or attachment needs, they will inevitably try to take care of their own needs at the exclusion of their partner, or rigidly demand that their partner meet all of their needs, and get very upset when they don't. Also remember that narcissists tend to suppress and numb emotion, which blocks the channel through which empathy can flow. This does not mean they are not capable of empathy. They're just blocked in being able to feel empathy because they aren't allowing themselves to access strong emotions.

There is a reason why many therapists struggle with narcissistic clients. For therapists who've ever had a narcissist in their life, it may arouse painful memories from their own personal experiences (negative countertransference). But if we, as clinicians, are to gain any traction in the therapy room, we have to find a way to empathize with them and offer them hope.

Borderline personality disordered clients

Remember that attachment theory gives us a framework for understanding human behavior and how people regulate (or dysregulate) their emotions. Borderline Personality Disorder (BPD) is the painted picture of disorganized attachment.[17,18] I have yet to meet someone with BPD that doesn't have some sort of attachment trauma. Most commonly, I have found that among those with BPD, the theme was having attachment figures who were inconsistent and unreliable. These attachment figures would offer love and affection some moments, but would revoke and withdraw it in the next moment, leaving the client emotionally confused and disoriented, never really able to make sense of what would trigger the entrance or exit of love and care.

This type of caregiving relationship can give birth to BPD,[18] and start reactive strategies of trial and error as they attempt to figure out what's going on in their attachment environment. This trial and error, a kind of experimental behavior to see if they can get a sense of what is what, can often be viewed as erratic on the outside. They don't mean to be erratic, and when you look at their attachment frame, it makes perfect sense that they would try to figure out what's happening in their world when their loved ones aren't available enough to help give them clarity.

This pattern also happens in their adult relationships, in which their romantic partner might tell them everything is great and secure one moment and then break up with them the next. Think of how unsettling that would be; how that would feel? To never truly know whether the one you love would be there for you. He or she would also never give you any warning sign or indication as to what would cause them to revoke their love and attention, or what it was that brought them back. It's like having nothing to emotionally anchor to. This can become the type of reinforcing behaviors that make it so hard for people with BPD to trust.

On the outside, the core features, or diagnostic criteria of BPD, according to the DSM-V,[16] are: heightened mood reactivity; emotional dysregulation; unstable self-image; constant fear of abandonment and frantic efforts to avoid such; impulsivity in areas like spending, sex, substance abuse, binge eating, and reckless driving; threats of self-harm; frequently displaying inappropriate or intense anger; and unstable and intense interpersonal relationships, often switching between idealizing or devaluing their relationship.[16]

My hope is that as you read over the above DSM diagnostic criteria you're already seeing these symptoms through the lens of attachment. On paper, it may be easier to see BPD through the eyes of attachment, but when you're in session, things can feel a lot different.

BPD can look like, in session, a client that presents themselves like they know it all, usually because they have read lots of books and articles in an effort to make sense of their attachment surroundings. These clients feel their emotions very intensely, which is beautiful in a way. They give everything their all, which can be great when you're in their good graces, but harsh when you fall out.

BPD clients can also present as rigid and defensive, trying to maintain control at all times of how therapy and their relationships go, trying to control the flow of interaction so that they can stay ahead of any possible danger. I've found that these clients are extremely sensitive and get very upset if they perceive the therapy session isn't going the way they anticipated. When their fear is triggered, they get highly reactive (the trauma response). They get highly agitated and can appear very defensive. But once the nervous system stops flooding the neural pathways, a different type of fear sets in. The fear that comes with remorse, the "what have I done" type of suddenly flipping into panicked apologizing, anxious emails or calls, all as an attempt to restore the connection. If they don't get a response to this new immediate threat, they flip back into the danger of rejection and that threat takes off.

I also find that these clients often describe feeling like they're going out of their mind in their relationships because no matter what they try, they just can't seem to get a secure bond from their attachment figures. They also describe doing a lot of work in their relationships. But their work is focused more on avoiding rejection and abandonment via a variety of strategies that really only band-aid a situation and don't provide lasting change or relief. Combined with the seemingly hair trigger trauma responses to threats, as described above, they aren't able to create lasting change and end up usually driving others away even further.

I think of people with BPD as marionette masters. They have a lot of strings moving all the time that they must constantly keep track of and attempt to control. Because they've not had secure attachment, and because they never really know how to make heads or tails as to whether an attachment figure is coming or going, these clients have to use a variety of strategies to try to keep attachment relationships nearby. Because they've had attachment trauma, they have no way to trust that others love them and will truly be there for them in a way they can securely rely on. They constantly fear abandonment or rejection. They are hypersensitive and extremely tuned into these cues. When someone is tuned in to this degree, they may detect and interpret a signal as possible rejection or abandonment (even though it is not). Because of the attachment trauma, people with BPD must constantly be on the lookout for signs of rejection or abandonment so that they can swiftly move into some action that might prevent that from happening.

This hypervigilance involves pulling emotional strings in a variety of ways to ensure that people stay close. This may include excessively pleasing others to the point where they have no boundaries and compromise their own values and integrity to maintain a relationship. For example, being a constant caregiver and excessively going above and beyond for others in an attempt to create such an overabundance of care that the receiver would never want to live without. They may also get upset and angry when they do jump through all of these hoops and it doesn't end up resulting in a secure bond. Also, because they're hypervigilant, if they start to detect that they will be rejected, they will push away their attachment figure as a way to avoid rejection. It is very consistent with disorganized attachment.[18]

People with BPD are also extremely smart and adaptive. They expend a lot of energy trying to keep all of the chess pieces on the board by anticipating every possible move and having a counter strategy waiting. It can feel manipulative, and often in couples therapy, their partners will complain that they feel manipulated. The person will use whatever strategy is best suited to the situation to keep people close or to keep people from leaving them or rejecting them. If they sense they are going to be rejected, however, they might even try to beat someone to the punch and reject them first so that they aren't the one being rejected.

Sometimes even as the therapist of someone with BPD, we can feel like we're on the receiving end of this. They may demand we do therapy a certain way, and may attack us if we don't comply. When these strategies are used, even though in the client's heart they just want to be loved or accepted, they don't have a healthy or effective means of getting that secure attachment bond. Eventually things fall apart, which reinforces their need to use these protective strategies. They are caught in a never-ending loop.

The double bind for someone with BPD is that because they are constantly maneuvering the emotional pieces or pulling on the puppet strings to try to avoid abandonment or rejection, they can never really be sure of a person's intentions when they do come close. They beckon people to come close, yet keep them away at the same time. They don't allow others to get too close because when they start to feel really vulnerable, their internal alarm goes off. So they often push others away at a point where it would be beneficial and positive for the relationship to get close and deepen the connection. This happens even in the therapy room, which can be frustrating for the therapist when we see their real pain, the bind they're in, but they won't allow us emotionally close enough to help them heal.

Another part of this double bind they're in is that they're really not sure if the people around them are there because they truly care about them, or because they're taking advantage of the nice things they are doing or providing for their loved one. But relaxing in their strategies and not doing these things is extremely risky, as it opens up the possibility that the other person really is only there for superficial reasons and not because they really love and value them.

> The risk in stopping these elaborate strategies is the other person confirming their worst fear: that they aren't really loved or valued.

The risk is too great. So they don't stop their strategies, they don't let their guard down. But they also get resentful that they're working so hard and no one is seeing how hard they're working to please, and they're getting no emotional credit for it. Hence where their anger springs up, which may feel inappropriate on the outside, actually isn't inappropriate at all. If we knew what was going on in their heart at the moment, we might really understand and empathize with what their anger is all about.

Conversely, much of the time, these defensive strategies can feel overwhelming and intrusive to other people, who end up reacting by pushing the person away, which in turn reinforces their greatest fear and the need to keep these strategies going. This is another example of the never-ending loop they're caught up in.

When I see BPD through the attachment lens, my heart really aches for the client. But before I learned to view it through the attachment lens, I would get triggered and really defensive when their reactive strategies would activate in session, and they'd start to verbally attack me. It is disturbing when a client verbally attacks you, even if you believe they're completely off base. I didn't know how to really see them through their pain and show up for them; I was caught up in their reactive behavior, which hijacked my empathy.

Once I saw these clients through the attachment lens, my heart shifted. I was able to see that people with BPD desperately need to have their attachment scars acknowledged and validated. They really need someone to see their hurt, and make sense of their behavior as an attempt to avoid rejection and abandonment.[18] For example, I once had a client, I'll call her Claire, who wouldn't stop her reactive maneuvers, even in therapy, until she felt like I was really with her, and even then she still didn't quite trust it at first. She didn't know how to trust. Like many other clients with BPD, she desperately wanted to be seen as working hard and willing to work hard for relationships with others. Once this all came together for me, I was able to climb back into the empathy window, and maintain relentless empathy throughout our work together. The more Claire felt empathized with, the more willing she was to be vulnerable and take emotional risks in session, and eventually also out of session, working toward building secure attachment bonds.

I think the most challenging part of working with someone with BPD for me is their rejection of my attempts to help them. This can feel super frustrating. When I was a new therapist, I remember thinking, "I get you, I'm here to help, why won't you let me close enough to help you?" But remember to stay in the attachment frame, which helps us maintain our relentless empathy. The client's rejection of our help doesn't reflect on our ability as a therapist. It's a symptom of their general distrust of others. This is why they don't let us get close sometimes; it feels scary, they feel vulnerable, and they're unsure if it's safe to let their guard down.

Therapeutic directions

Whether we see a personality disordered client for individual or couples therapy, real change won't be possible unless we can show relentless empathy for them. If we can look underneath the reactive strategies and get curious as to the attachment trauma that birthed these behaviors, then we have a better chance of touching the heart of their humanness, and that's where we stand the greatest chance of them being open and willing to change.

When a couple comes in for therapy and one partner insists the other is personality disordered, what you as the therapist should be assessing is their ability to feel and regulate emotions and their attachment history. In the case of narcissism, the therapist can work on helping the narcissist to feel their emotions, to allow themselves to make contact with their own inner emotional world and the world of their partner. You could ask the narcissistic partner, "What would it be like to make room in your world for your partner's emotions? To allow your partner's emotions to impact or touch you in some way?" If they are presenting for couples counseling, as defensive and as cool as they may play it, they are there for a reason. They could have just walked away and not even tried. Even showing up is an act of vulnerability, a peek behind the façade of a narcissist.

Therapy with someone with a personality disorder should not be about trying to pry their defenses out of their hands; it should not involve trying to cognitively explain how bad their behavior is and talk them out of acting that way. This is the wrong approach. Vulnerability is extremely hard for these clients. Clients with BPD can be more vocal about their emotional pain, but they often don't know how to express their pain in a healthy way.

For narcissists, their key strategy is emotional avoidance, so you need to intervene on the emotional level, and you cannot do that by working only on the cognitive level. This goes for all clients, personality disordered or not. The therapy session must be emotionally experiential, helping the client make contact with their deeper emotions, and to start expanding their window of tolerance for emotional experiencing and vulnerability.

In EFT we have a strategy whereby we don't strip people of their defenses; we hand their defenses to them. The goal is to validate the functionality of the emotions driving the behavioral responses (not validating the behavior but the strategy underneath). By doing this we can more easily join with the client, build a positive alliance, and stand with them as we help them to put down their own defenses.

For narcissists, the bottom line is if they want to maintain their relationships, they have to make room for others. This cannot be done without first helping them to be more comfortable tolerating their own emotions as well as the emotions of others. But regardless of the client or the personality disorder, creating emotional safety through new safe emotional experiences in the therapy room (and hopefully eventually in the outside world as well) will allow us to help them start expanding their attachment frame and to learn how to rely on others in a healthy way.

Remember, relying on others does not mean one cannot do things for themselves. It means that we can access our partner as a safe space to help us regulate our emotions, through co-regulation, which neuroscience has shown has a far more beneficial effect on the nervous system than trying to do this process on our own. We are talking about secure, healthy interdependence, which *promotes connection and bonding*.[13]

When working with a narcissist, helping them make room for others means the client has to learn how to take emotional risks to allow someone else to be there for them, something they usually avoid. Allowing someone else to be there for them means they have to stop coming to their own rescue. By allowing their partner to come close instead of always relying on only themselves, they're able to deepen their emotional connectivity and strengthen their attachment bond. This means vulnerability. Helping them be emotionally vulnerable with their partner will also help them learn how to emotionally be there for their partner when their partner is emotionally vulnerable.

We should work on shaping vulnerability in session, helping it to not feel so scary or risky. When the therapist can help a narcissist learn to make more contact with their emotions, the channels of empathy will open up.

When clients feel our emotional presence through relentless empathy, the therapeutic relationship stands the best chance of helping to create channels for growth, healing, and change.[13]

Questions to consider

1. What is your personal view of personality disorders?
2. How can you see personality disorders differently through the lens of attachment?
3. Think of any challenging or difficult clients you might have had that presented with a personality disorder. As you now see them through the lens of attachment, what would you have done differently?
4. What interventions will you do differently going forward using what you've learned from this chapter?

Notes

1 History of the term, Borderline Personality Disorder. www.verywellmind.com/borderline-personality-disorder-meaning-425191
2 Trauma and personality disorders. Blizard, R. (1997). The origins of dissociative identity disorder from an object relations and attachment theory perspective. *Dissociation: Progress in the Dissociative Disorders*, X: 223–229.
3 Trauma and personality disorders. Brothers, D. (2014). Traumatic attachments: Intergenerational trauma, dissociation, and the analytic relationship. *International Journal of Psychoanalytic Self Psychology*, 9(1): 3–15.
4 Trauma and borderline personality disorder. Golier., J. A., Yehuda, R., Bierer, L., Mitropoulou, M. A., New, A. S., Schmeidler, J., Silverman, J., & Sierver, L. J. (2003). The relationship of borderline personality disorder to posttraumatic stress disorder

and traumatic events. *The American Journal of Psychiatry, 160*(11): 2018–2024.
5 Trauma and the origin of personality disorders. Ogle, C. M., Rubin, D. C., & Siegler, I. C. (2015). The relation between insecure attachment and posttraumatic stress: Early life versus adulthood traumas. *Psychological Trauma: Theory, Research, Practice, and Policy, 7*(4): 324–332.
6 Trauma, attachment and personality disorders. Blizard, R. A. (2003). Disorganized attachment, development of dissociated self states, and a relational approach to treatment. *Journal of Trauma & Dissociation, 4*(3): 27–50.
7 Attachment trauma and personality disorders. Lyons-Ruth, K. (2008). Contributions of the mother-infant relationship to dissociative, borderline, and conduct symptoms in young adulthood. *Infant Mental Health Journal, 29*(3): 203–218.
8 Neglect, attachment trauma and personality disorders. Wright, M., Crawford, E., & Del Castillo, D. (2009). Childhood emotional maltreatment and later psychological distress among college students: The mediating role of maladaptive schemas. *Journal of Child Abuse and Neglect, 33*(1): 59–68.
9 Maté, G. (2012). Addiction: Childhood trauma, stress and the biology of addiction. *Journal of Restorative Medicine, 1*(1): 56–63.
10 Trauma and pain. (2019). Gabor Matè. https://drgabormate.com/opioids-universal-experience-addiction/
11 Crawford, T. N., Livesley, W. J., & Jang, K. L. (2007). Insecure attachment and personality disorder: A twin study of adults. *European Journal of Personality, 21*: 191–208.
12 Meyer, B., & Pilkonis, P. A. (2005). An attachment model of personality disorders. In: M. F. Lenzenweger & J. F. Clarkin (Eds.), *Major theories of personality disorder* (pp. 231–281). New York, NY: The Guilford Press.
13 Johnson, S. M. (2019). *Attachment theory in practice: Emotionally focused therapy with individuals, couples and families.* New York, NY: The Guilford Press.
14 Narcissus Greek Mythology. (2019). Encyclopædia Britannica, inc. www.britannica.com/topic/Narcissus-Greek-mythology
15 History of Narcissism. Rhodewalt, F. (2018). Narcissism. Encyclopædia Britannica, inc.
16 American Psychiatric Association. (2013). *Diagnostic and statistical manual of mental disorders* (5th ed.). Arlington, VA: Author.
17 Scott, L. N., Levy, K. N., & Pincus, A. L. (2009). Adult attachment, personality traits, and borderline personality disorder features in young adults. *Journal of Personality Disorders, 23*(3): 258–280.
18 Levy, K. N. (2005). The implications of attachment theory and research for understanding borderline personality disorder. *Journal of Development and Psychopathology, 17*(4): 959–968.

Chapter 5

Relentless empathy for addicted clients

> The question is not why the addiction, but why the pain.
> Gabor Matè[1]

Many researchers and doctors subscribe to the definition of addiction as any behavior or substance a person uses to find temporary relief, pleasure, or soothing/comfort, alter states of being, that suffers negative consequences and can't give up.[1] This could be alcohol or drugs, shopping, sex, gambling, video games, or work, for example. Clinicians and doctors usually view addiction as the problem, but for those with the addiction, it is their solution. When understanding someone's struggle with addiction, as Gabor Matè so aptly says, we need to be looking at not why the addiction, but what is the person's pain that the addiction has become the solution to.

One of the most significant barriers I've noticed to having empathy for those with addiction is our own view of addicts and addiction. It can be easy to write people off and label them as junkies or bums. That their addiction is just about wanting to have fun or party all the time. We might pass an addict on the streets, ignoring their streetside begging, and failing to see them as human beings. This is the thing: they are human beings. There is no dignity in begging for money with a cardboard sign on the freeway exit. There is no glory in that. Can you imagine, for a moment, how low a person has had to fall, to be in that place? But pathologizing addiction is another way that we lose empathy for those that struggle with it. Without relentless empathy here, we can lose sight of the human being and only see the addiction.

Another part of the problem with having empathy for addicted clients is in how we have traditionally thought of addiction as a whole. Societally speaking, we also don't have a great setup for viewing addiction. The law that guides our societal definition of addiction says it's a choice that people make, and therefore they must be punished.[1] The law fails to see the human being in pain using the addiction as a way out of their pain. We punish people and make them criminals for suffering and trying to cope with their pain instead of helping them find alternative solutions. We can't punish the pain out of people. It just isn't effective.

The other view society tends to take toward addiction is the medical model, which says it's a genetic or medical disease that people suffer from,[1] yet attempts to medicate people away from addiction also haven't worked, likely because when people see themselves as sick they're putting blame on their illness and taking responsibility for their behavior. Addiction is in actuality neither of these. It's a human life problem. And research clearly states insecure attachment is at the base of nearly all those who suffer from addiction.[2,3] If we can't understand and see addiction for what it truly is, then it will be more difficult to maintain relentless empathy for people who suffer from addiction.

What makes working with addicts so challenging? From my experience working at an addiction center in Lower Manhattan, and from what other clinicians in the field have shared with me, addiction is so hard because it requires so much work to quit. Not everyone who enters into addiction treatment makes it into recovery. Relapse is very common among people with addiction, which can become frustrating and discouraging for clinicians, as well as family and friends of the addict. Sometimes these clients suffer more than one relapse. Many people drop out of treatment. Sometimes, the worst case happens, and clients pass away due to overdose.

Another complication is the impact of addiction on other people's lives, on the lives of the families of addicts, on the therapists who try to help them, and even the addict themselves. The effects are painful and frustrating, and often very destructive. What can be equally frustrating is the family of the addict that thinks they are helping the addict by dancing around their addiction, thereby enabling it to continue. These family members refuse to be a part of the solution by removing temptations or triggers for the addict. Their mentality is that they aren't struggling with addiction, so they are free to engage in substance use in the presence of the addict because they don't abuse it or aren't addicted to it. So therapists are caught trying to help a client with addiction within a system that's setting them up for failure and relapse. This can lead to a myopic view of the addiction and behavior itself rather than the human underneath the addiction.

When we fail to see the humanness in the addict, we lose empathy. When we write a person off as "just another addict," we enter into a frame of hopelessness and start seeing the person as incapable of change. Recovering from addiction may be a long and bumpy road, but it is totally within the realm of possibility. Having empathy for this journey requires more patience, more humanness, and more energy invested in creating relentless empathy.

Addiction and attachment

There is a strong relationship between addiction and attachment.[2,3] Disrupted early attachment bonding, necessitating adaptive survival mechanisms, when left unresolved, can become barriers to emotional flexibility and bonding in relationships. When people were not taught emotional regulation and soothing in the context of secure attachment bonding, it leaves them more vulnerable to turning to unhealthy alternatives such as substances or compulsive behaviors to soothe and escape. Fundamentally, failed development of secure attachment creates an attachment to survival mechanisms and defenses such as substances and/or other compulsive behaviors in an attempt to find comfort, soothing, emotion regulation, happiness, escape, and a sense of control.[2]

Even the medical profession has discovered that attachment disruptions in early childhood alter a child's stress mechanisms and impact how they react to and cope with stress later in life.[1] Furthermore, these altered stress mechanisms from early trauma and attachment disruption create more sensitivity to pain, and therefore more defenses needed to block the pain. Addicts lack the ability to internally self-regulate their emotions and frequently turn to substances or acting out compulsive behaviors to regulate pain and emotional experiences. They turn to addictions to calm and soothe, numb out uncomfortable or unpleasant emotional experiences or memories, or create feelings of pleasure and euphoria. Even non-chemical substances such as pornography and gambling are demonstrated to have similar effects on the brain as chemical substances. They can be used by a person to achieve the same effect.

At the heart of it, addiction is all about attachment.[1,2,3] If you look hard enough, dig deep enough in the history of an addict, you'll find broken or disrupted attachment bonds. Sometimes these are one-time events that have a powerful and pervasive effect on a person's life. Sometimes they are more subtle and insidious in a client's life like a slow leaky faucet, one little drip at a time. Sometimes their family does simply not teach them how to deal with adversity, that someone can be there for them through hard times, and at some point find their way into addiction. Many times it may start off as an attempt to elevate and intensify feelings of excitement and pleasure, and minimize boredom and loneliness or other emotional discomfort, but then eventually becomes a primary way of trying to get through daily life.

When we fall in love, our brain produces a variety of chemicals: oxytocin, vasopressin, and dopamine. Oxytocin and vasopressin are hormones associated with bonding and long-term attachment, while dopamine stimulates the reward center of the brain. Those that don't have safe or secure relationships to stimulate these natural chemicals in their brains must find alternative strategies to meet the same end. Euphoria-inducing drugs such as cocaine, and even alcohol, can stimulate pleasure and reward centers in the brain; however, they aren't as long-lasting as the natural chemical releases we get from bonding and secure love relationships. In a 2011 UCSF study on fruit flies,[4] researchers found that male fruit flies who were sexually rejected drank four times as much alcohol than those who were able to mate. The alcohol stimulates the same part of their brain, but it's a different way of getting there.

Relationship problems and addiction also go hand in hand. When people don't have secure attachment to begin with, they are already vulnerable to turning to addiction as a way to manage painful emotions and coping with stress. Coming into a relationship with such coping strategies, these strategies are likely to stay in place (without therapy or interventions). When distress happens in the relationship, as it happens in all relationships at one point or another, the addicted partner may attempt to minimize this distress by again using their insecure attachment strategies such as turning outside of the relationship to the addiction to self-soothe the pain, or to find alternate ways of getting emotional needs met. Ironically, the word "addiction" actually comes from a Latin word meaning "a devoting" (*addictionem*).[5] In Roman times, addiction was a person who became enslaved according to law, which is interesting as addiction can be thought of as a form of enslavement.[5]

Sometimes within relationships, couples will use recreational drugs together as a way to connect, but in reality, they are both checking out together. The term "recreational" as well is important because many couples do not consider recreational drug use an addiction or a problem. Additionally, this recreational usage is a buffer, or a substitute for actual emotional engagement because neither person knows how to, or at least doesn't feel safe, bonding without a mask or a buffer. So recreational usage becomes an illusion of connection. And in reality, if people knew how to authentically bond and deeply connect together, that connection would provide a better high than the substances!

Because substances and compulsive behaviors have been shown to have analgesic (pain-blocking chemicals released in the brain) effects, which aid in the numbing out of emotionally painful experiences and situations, they can easily become a substitute for human connection.[3] Addiction doesn't create a connection between people; it actually isolates people and increases disconnection from others. The irony is that many people turn to addiction as a way to cope with feeling isolated and disconnected from others. The addiction thereby becomes an enabling mechanism for this system of disconnection from others to continue and stay in place.[2] Sometimes people themselves are aware of it; many times, they're quite in denial of it. This is another reason that working with addiction is so challenging. Because despite the obvious negative consequences happening in the addict's life, many are in complete denial of these consequences. So if a client is in denial that there's a problem, how do they end up in treatment?

Addicts enter into treatment for all sorts of reasons. Some people with addiction only come because it is mandatory by court order, as was the majority of the cases of clients I saw at the facility in Manhattan. Others come in because of pressure from their spouses or family, or some enter into treatment because they want to break the chains of their addiction.

In my experience working with addicts, many of them do not suffer negative consequences, at least, consequences that either they don't recognize as negative, or aren't negative *enough* to motivate them toward recognizing their use as a problem. That didn't mean the person wasn't addicted, however. I believe this is the most difficult aspect of working with addiction.

True to the nature of addiction, addicts usually live in denial that there's a problem. The person may already be experiencing negative consequences, like more frequent fights with their spouse over their addiction, or getting a DUI, or lowered workplace performance. But because these consequences haven't resulted in life-altering consequences and are perceived by the addict as only minor annoyances, it didn't result in a change in perception about their addiction. For an addict who hasn't suffered negative consequences, often, it's easier for them to blame others for being upset about their substance use than it is to see their use as a problem.

These types of addicts become the most challenging to work with, as it is difficult for the treating clinician to maintain relentless empathy. Therapists and addiction counselors can get frustrated, overwhelmed, stressed out, discouraged, or feel a sense of helplessness to get their addicted clients to a place of freedom from addiction. Being in this frame can make it very tempting for the addiction therapist to shut down and avoid their own emotional responses toward their clients because it takes too much energy to feel care and compassion for someone who clearly is not interested in changing their addiction.

Many people find themselves in the throes of addiction to escape from pain, a sense of control, relief from loneliness, or inner peace (lowered anxiety).[3] In this way, addiction was not the problem, but the perceived solution to a problem.[1] Addiction can be viewed as an attempt to solve a problem. Those with insecure attachment are more likely to be vulnerable to turning to substance or behavioral addictions (sometimes called process addictions) as a way to control or cope with stress and problems. Those with secure attachment are more likely to use healthy strategies to solve their most difficult problems. They are more likely to find healthy ways of regulating their emotional states that are flexible to meet the demands of the situation and are not rigidly set.

How in a world of 7 billion people did someone come to feel lonely? How did someone come to lack the agency to be in control of their decisions and choices? Why are we in so much emotional pain? These questions are just variations of emotional pain.

We should be asking our clients what happened in their life that they feel pain or distress, and have come to attempt to solve these problems with an addiction, and how can we help the person solve this problem in another way?

Another complication is clients that claim they don't have any pain or anything major in their life that has happened that they can correlate their addiction with. Sometimes this is because they are so numb from the addiction and can't register pain. I find this is also common among clients that suffered from emotional neglect, where maybe they weren't abused or hit, nor had anything physically traumatic happen to them, but from a young age, they were left to their own devices to find happiness, entertainment, and solve problems on their own, often leading them into trouble. Though they've learned to survive on their own, once boredom or loneliness kicks in, they turn to pleasure-inducing activities or substances, *not human connection*. Where parental connection and involvement would have significantly helped influence their child to make healthy and productive decisions, kids found solutions in unhealthy ways and often from sources or people that were unhealthy and emotionally damaged as well.[1] Eventually, they formed a bond with their addiction or behavior. This bond became a substitute for human connection.

Many of my clients that use euphoria-inducing drugs fall into this category. As a way to experience happiness and pleasure, they found their way into substances or process addictions such as video games, gambling, or pornography. As children, my clients have described being left to their own devices and turning to their neighborhood friends who had an older sibling or a parent that either drank, smoked, used recreational or prescription drugs, or allowed children to party and use alcohol. Some of these clients just wanted to be accepted by their peers. Not having any consistent and regular emotional connection at home, the addicted client as a child gave into peer pressure so that they could feel a sense of acceptance and belonging with the only ones seemingly offering it in their social environment.

Emotional neglect is very insidious in the development of addiction. Many don't realize that neglect can also send a powerful signal to people about their value in the world. Because of neglect, many people grew up feeling like they weren't wanted. Remember that emotional contact shapes the quality of our attachment relationships, and attachment shapes our neurology and physiology, all of which shape our brain functions. In this type of environment, and without secure attachment, it becomes challenging for people to develop healthy and lasting ways to experience true joy and happiness, so they chase euphoria using certain types of drugs or behaviors. In the case of my clients and those of my colleagues, 100% of these clients had insecure attachment. Some of them used these euphoric drugs as a substitute for their lack of attachment, many of them being completely attachment avoidant. Without consistent, secure human connection, how can people naturally experience happiness that is lasting? For them, it's only been momentary, much like the drugs they use.

Some of our addicted clients have experienced unwanted sexual acts at a young age, opening the door to other kinds of emotionally disconnected sexual experiences later in life. Many clients walked away from those experiences with a sense that sex was not an intimate act of connection and bonding, but just a behavior to have an orgasm. On one end, people may use it as another form of a pleasure-inducing drug, while others learn it is an avenue through which they attempt to get emotional needs met, such as belonging or acceptance or love.

As clinicians, if we can tune into the painful messages that our addicted client received at some point during their life, it will be easier to understand what we're working with and maintain our empathy.

Case examples

I had an addicted client, we'll call him Tom, who was neglected as a child. His parents were busy all the time, both working two jobs, and in their off time, they drank alcohol or went to social gatherings with their friends. At the age of 6, Tom's father passed away from a tragic car accident, and Tom's mother gave him up for foster care because she was unable to care for him. While it was out of love for her child that she gave Tom up, at an early age, Tom got the message he wasn't wanted. While he did find a nice foster care family, his foster parents had three other children, and like his biological parents, both worked two jobs and didn't spend much of their downtime connecting with the children. The other children in the home treated Tom like an outsider, which only reinforced his feelings of not being wanted.

Tom found a sense of belonging by running errands and trimming the grass for the elderly lady who lived next door for a few dollars each week. Tom grew up to become a physician's assistant and workaholic, an addiction which is also hard for people to own as a problem because of the positive rewards that come with working a lot of hours, such as large paychecks. Additionally, in order to keep up with the work demand, Tom had started using opioids. Over time, he didn't realize how often he started relying on opioids to get him through. Tom's wife started to feel neglected and unwanted herself and ended up having an affair ten years into their marriage. This affair nearly broke Tom, and triggered, once again, his feelings of not being wanted. His opioid addiction ramped up and almost cost him his career.

In our work together, we were able to identify the pain Tom felt, how he was able to numb out, and use work and opioids as his escape. As we mapped his attachment history, we identified how he learned the only attachment relationship available to him was one in which he was caring for others. The value of caring for others meant that Tom would guarantee a sense of being wanted and needed. This is how he came to become a physician's assistant, a job where the sick and dying are in no short supply and are always in need of care. While he was busy trying to meet his need to feel wanted and needed at work, he failed to see how much he was wanted and needed by his wife at home. This paved the way for this growing ravine of isolation and loneliness in their marriage, which left his wife vulnerable to feeling cared for by another. And though Tom was seeking relief through caring for patients and using opioids, he described feeling a constant sense of loneliness and isolation.

Through our work together, Tom was able to connect the dots between his early attachment experiences as well as his needs and longings with his behavior and coping strategies. He was able to set boundaries with work and stop his opioid usage as he learned healthy ways of getting his needs met. He was able to repair his relationship with his wife, and they were able to build a better and more secure connection together over time.

Another client, let's call her Julie, was sexually molested at the age of 12 by her older brother's best friend in the upstairs loft while her parents were down in their basement having a party and getting drunk. Her parents were both functional alcoholics and not emotionally available. Around the same time, she was frequently bullied by her peers for not having "the right look" because her family spent their money on alcohol instead of new clothes for the kids. When Julie came to see me in her late 20s, it was clear Julie had become addicted to sex, an addiction that manifested itself in increasingly risky sexual acts and encounters with people who were not intimately known to Julie (finding anonymous partners online and in clubs). Julie had had several STDs in her life, was raped and robbed of her possessions during one of these encounters, gotten pregnant and put the baby up for adoption (which she regretted), she even had her fiancé, who was addicted to drugs, run security for her while she had these encounters in hotel rooms.

Julie had seen other therapists at various points in her life because of the deep sense of shame she felt, yet still could not stop herself from turning to these encounters. Early on in our sessions, I asked Julie, "Has anyone ever mentioned sex addiction to you?" Her facial expression changed as if to show "Eureka" as she replied, "no, not ever!"

As we traced Julie's attachment history and connected the dots with her sexual behavior, what we uncovered was that Julie received an important message about herself as a 12-year-old that started that night in her upstairs loft. The message she got about herself was that she was only wanted for her body, that people were only interested in her when she was sexually available. She had a hard time really letting people emotionally close to her even though she had a large social network. No matter how many sexual partners she had, she still felt empty. Something that another therapist had described as "sexual liberation" was actually an attachment message that only through sexual acts, only for her body, was she wanted and felt valued. So Julie learned to use her body and sex as a way to feel wanted ... to feel good enough as a person.

As Julie was able to see the connection between her behavior and her early trauma and attachment experiences, she was able to learn healthy and effective strategies for getting her needs for love and acceptance met. She was able to construct a healthier, attachment-based outlook on sex, and recognize her own worth and value as a person. As she learned to regulate her own emotions, she was able to set better boundaries. As her self-esteem developed and became healthy, she was able to form new and secure bonds with others, both with friends and romantic relationships. Her recovery even inspired her parents to get help. Eventually, they were able to build a new and closely connected, healthy family relationship.

Hope for addiction

All humans need to feel wanted. It is normal and healthy to want to feel wanted, though sometimes the behavioral method of getting this need met is not healthy. Remember, it is secure, healthy attachment that promotes and develops resilient and healthy coping strategies in the world. The problem with most current treatment approaches for addiction is that it attempts to stop the addiction by constricting a person's behavioral repertoire. The focus of these treatment modalities is on the wrong level. They're trying to change the outcome of the addiction and not the reason for the addiction. When clinicians can see the addiction through the attachment lens, they can help clients work on building secure, healthy attachment. Additionally, they can also help clients develop the ability to regulate negative emotions and more flexible ways of responding to pain or distress.

I have also had many clients that worked in drug treatment and recovery centers. These addiction programs tend to follow traditional addiction treatment protocol, which does not teach people how to feel emotions and effectively learn how to regulate them. They also don't teach addicts about vulnerability. If we don't teach the clients about either of these, as well as how to build a secure attachment system, then all we're doing when they enter recovery is stripping away their defense mechanisms for protecting themselves in these emotional places. As soon as they start feeling their emotions again (because their substance of choice is no longer blocking their emotional signals), then we've just stripped them of their defenses and left them emotionally naked without the tools or strategies to deal with the demons and dragons in the world. No wonder people relapse! Many of these treatment programs, in my opinion, set addicts up for failure.

We shouldn't be teaching them behavioral interventions alone; we should be teaching them about healthy attachment, emotion regulation, and how to truly connect with others and be vulnerable. Addiction is about isolation. The opposite of addiction is not sobriety, it's connection.

We're asking them to live emotionally naked and raw, without any protection. Of course that feels very risky and dangerous! They have not yet learned how to cope with feeling their own emotions, especially when they've not had many or any safe experiences of someone showing up for them in their pain and showing them love and acceptance. If we strip that away from them, before they've had a consistency of new experiences where they've had success feeling their emotions or having consistent, secure emotional contact, then they're virtually emotionally naked, raw, and exposed! No wonder giving up their addiction feels like such a bad idea! Addicts have had little success with vulnerability. And without their addiction, they have nothing to mask their pain, nothing to protect them from the pain they feel, or the inevitable rejection and abandonment they feel certain they'll receive.

It's important to keep this in the front of our hearts as we work with our addicted clients toward feeling their emotions, feeling their "feels" as people call it now, and helping them to experience vulnerability in a safe way, a new way that actually results in deeper connection and love. The more they have new safe emotional experiences in session, the easier it will become for them not to need to turn to addiction or behaviors to cope with their emotions or vulnerability.

The antidote to addiction is connection.[1]

Questions to consider

1. What is your personal viewpoint or belief about addiction?
2. How do you view addicts who come to you for treatment?
3. Have you been able to identify their emotional pain?
4. Have you been able to trace the history of their attachment patterns and relationships?

Notes

1 Maté, G. (2012). Addiction: Childhood trauma, stress and the biology of addiction. *Journal of Restorative Medicine*, 1(1): 56–63.
2 Attachment and addiction. Gill, R. (2014). *Addictions from an attachment perspective: Do broken bonds and early trauma lead to addictive behaviours?* London: Karnac.
3 Attachment and addiction. Flores, P. J. (2004). *Addiction as an attachment disorder*. Lanham: Jason Aronson, Inc.
4 UCSF Study on fruit flies and rejection. Shohat-Ophir, G., Kaun, K. R., Azanchi, R., Mohammed, H., & Heberlein, U. (2012). Sexual deprivation increases ethanol intake in Drosophila. *Science*, 335(6074): 1351–1355.
5 Rosenthal, R. J., & Faris, S. B. (2019). The etymology and early history of "addiction". *Addiction Research & Theory*, 27(5): 437–449.

Chapter 6

Relentless empathy for angry or hostile clients

> Relentless Empathy Corrodes Aggression.
>
> Dr. Susan Johnson

When working with clients, the one emotion I find therapists repeatedly say becomes the most triggering for them is anger. When clients get angry, they can get hostile in their words and tone. They may start verbally attacking their partner or their therapist in session, which usually sparks a reaction on the inside of everyone in the room. Anger, in general, when expressed, can alienate others who are on the receiving end of it. But relentless empathy for someone who's angry, as reflected in the words of Sue Johnson above, can have a powerful impact.

A lot of therapists get dysregulated by the heat of anger. When this happens, there seem to be two ways in which our threat detection gets activated: either the client gets angry at their spouse in session, prompting our instinct to protect the wounded partner or spouse. The second is when the clients direct their anger toward us as the therapists and start making us the object of their criticism and contempt.

When I was an intern therapist, I remember one of my first encounters with a client's anger in session. I was working with a couple trying to outline and understand their cycle of behavior in their pattern of distress. I remember as I was validating the husband's attachment needs, and making sense of how he would withdraw or appease to avoid his wife's rejection or criticism, the wife started to get really angry at both him and me. I remember her saying something to the effect of "that's not what happens" (while internally thinking *"clearly it is because it's happening right now!"*).

Then she turned to me and said, "What would you know?! You've known us for five minutes! This is such crap!" *Whoa!* I thought to myself. This was escalating out of control, and here I was, a newbie therapist terrified of upsetting a client out of fear they wouldn't come back. At that moment, I got triggered into my own defensiveness, which only worsened the client's angry responses.

When I got defensive, she didn't feel heard or understood. My fight or flight responses kicked in, and it hijacked my emotional presence and kept me from really leaning into her anger and making sense of her response. She got up and stormed out. The husband actually felt completely validated because this was exactly what happened continually between them at home. He was glad someone else was experiencing it and that he wasn't alone. Even though he felt completely validated, I still felt really bad on the inside. With couples, to lose one half isn't a win. I felt terrible, and I knew I didn't handle it the best way. Needless to say, this was a huge learning experience for me with working with anger, which my wonderful supervisor at the time really helped me process. But since then, I have come to learn that many new and seasoned therapists have found themselves in a similar situation at one point or another during their career.

Anger 101

The most important thing I ever learned about anger that forever changed my nervous system's appraisal of anger is this: Anger is an expression of pain or fear.[1] The more the anger, the deeper the pain, or the stronger the fear. The more the pain, the more sensitive and reactive the person is. Reactive behavior is an expression of pain. Reactive behavior is how a person behaves, or what they do when they feel emotions.[2] All emotions produce a reaction. Some people's reaction is to suppress the emotional responses, while others may ramp it up. These reactive strategies will, of course, vary depending on a person's attachment security (or lack thereof) and their fight or flight responses.[1]

> Anger is an expression of pain or fear. The more the anger, the deeper the pain, or the stronger the fear.

Angry behavior or angry vocal tones can immediately trigger our body's threat detection system[3] and light up that silent alarm on the inside (or maybe not so silent sometimes). A lot of therapists, like myself in the past, think the client's anger is a rejection of them and a criticism on their skills rather than something valuable and painful the client is trying to express. Expressions of anger can get expressed in a way that feels threatening. This is why without understanding what anger is really about, it's easy to get triggered by the client's anger.

Reactive behavior is a sign of threat according to the brain. And remember, emotional connection/disconnection from others is part of the brain's survival system. The more someone isn't heard or understood, the angrier they get. When people poke at you, underneath they're either really saying "I need to know you hear me and can help me" or "I'm not sure how to feel safe here" or "do you love or care for me enough to fight for me?" or they're saying "you really hurt me." The best thing I can do for another person is brave the fire of their vitriol and show up for them where they need me most. I've also learned that sometimes this is one of the hardest things to do.

Anger is also a sign of fear. Think about the parent whose young child wanders away in the grocery store and doesn't answer when called by name. Or the teen who stays out after curfew and doesn't call their parents to let them know they're safe. Many times the parents get really angry and might even scold their child, "Why did you do that?! You know better!" They're angry, but really, they were terrified for their child's safety. This fear can also show up in relationships when one person suddenly terminates the relationship unexpectedly. Anger is a common response to fear when predictability and connection are lost together. The adrenaline rush that comes over our body from anger during moments of fear mobilizes our body to, in this case, protect our loved ones.

Soldiers are trained to lean into their anger as a way to override their fear responses. The physiological response to fear is usually flight or freeze, which would actually lead to more harm on the battlefield; whereas anger mobilizes the body into action, which is extremely adaptive for survival situations such as war. Because war and warlike situations involve a systematic rewiring of the nervous system, it can be very difficult for soldiers to get their bodies out of this adaptive survival mode once they come home, even though they are back to a safe survival situation. The same can be said for police officers, whose lifespan after retirement is an average of five to six years.[4] They also, as a profession, suffer higher divorce rates usually related to anger management issues.[4]

Anger can also be a reactive, secondary emotion that protects something deeper and more vulnerable underneath. When exploring anger, I've often heard clients say they do feel hurt or sad underneath, but their past attempts to express their more vulnerable emotions were not successful, and they felt shut down, dismissed, or rejected by their partner or attachment figure.[1] So as the pain from not having their attachment figure be emotionally receptive and responsive to their hurt became more a regular experience, the clients at some point realize it's too painful to put themselves out there and share these vulnerable parts only to get rejected, completely misunderstood, shut down, or not responded to.

The anger of hope vs. the anger of despair

Anger has a function; it serves a purpose. Understanding how the anger is functioning for a particular person is an essential part of diffusing the intensity of the anger. Many therapists don't recognize that there is an anger of hope and an anger of despair. Both forms of anger may look critical or display hostility on the outside, but if you look closer, the anger of hope usually shows up more like an attempt to engage while the anger of despair more often tries to shut down connection and disengage.

Often anger will take over for deeper, more primary emotions and protect the hurt beneath a cloak of reactive "this isn't fair" type of angry responses. Now instead of directly presenting their deeper, more vulnerable hurts, they would poke, attack, criticize, blame, interrogate, and a whole litany of angry behaviors that clearly didn't have the intended effect they were hoping. But when we unpack these types of angry responses, if you ask a client what would happen if they didn't get angry and poke, we find that clients will often say "if I don't get angry then nothing will change, and I'll never get my needs met, I'll never be understood, or I won't matter to my partner." So while their deeper, primary emotions have given up hope, their anger has taken over and helps them continue to fight for their voice, for the relationship. Their anger in this way is still their hope that something could still be different.

However, sometimes, this anger becomes so intense from prolonged unprocessed hurt that a partner no longer has hope of things changing and stops using their anger as a way to fight for change. This can be called the anger of despair; the angry part of a person that has given up hope for change, hope for the relationship on all fronts, and they are in a place where their anger helps them detach and tries to get their partner to back off or go away from trying to repair the relationship. Their anger is now a distancing behavior. This type of anger can become very destructive in its intensity and may become intentionally injurious to their partner, and could lead to violence or death.

Anger as a protector and advocator

Anger is a very adaptive emotion. It helps us protect and/or advocate for ourselves. Anger arouses our reactive defense system. The strength of the reactivity we see is tantamount to the depth of the client's pain. This is often why you see kids, even adults, act out with anger and aggression as a way to communicate the pain inside where words have otherwise failed to convey the point.

Anger is primarily a reaction to a perceived threat from an outside force. It can help protect us from aggressors. When we get angry, our body is flooded with adrenaline and norepinephrine, which helps mobilize the brain and body for action. When our threat response system comes online, and our defenses are activated, the brain automatically shuts down our social engagement system as it prepares for survival.[3]

As an advocator, anger can help us stand up for ourselves, to help us fight to be heard, or to help us attempt to get our needs met. When in advocator mode, anger can help us feel empowered, strong, in control, and speak for ourselves when otherwise we might not have the courage to speak up. Anger can help us advocate for felt injustices, to speak up against a sense of "unfairness." Sometimes after prolonged periods of feeling hurt, not feeling understood, or feeling ignored, feelings shift to anger, which helps us keep fighting for ourselves or our relationships when the hurt parts have started to feel hopeless.

I once asked the million-dollar question to one of my angry clients in their couples therapy session, "What would happen if you didn't get angry?" Their response helped me understand the function of their anger. The angry partner replied, "then I wouldn't exist; I wouldn't matter." Without anger, my client would go to a much darker place. Their anger was functioning as an advocator to keep fighting to feel like they matter to their partner; to feel like there's a chance their partner would hear them, and they could get their needs met. There is something healthy and beautiful about that, even though the behavior isn't effective in getting their partner to come closer.

This shows up in the couples I work with, where one partner reacts with angry protest when their partner shuts down or withdraws. Most of the time, angry partners will describe having tried multiple "calmer" ways of getting through to their partners but have been met with little or no success. Trying to reach a loved one about hurt or conflict, only to have them not respond, shut down, or walk away can activate the brain's threat detection system, arousing angry emotions that activate the body and mobilize it to fight to keep their partner connected.

This behavior may look like blame, accusations, verbal poking or jabbing, interrogations, frequent texting, or even other following behavior. For most of my clients that are in the protesting position in their relationship conflict patterns, this angry protest feels like a much better option than doing nothing. In their shoes, if they didn't get angry and fight, if they did nothing, then nothing would happen. In fact, their partner would likely continue to pull away, resulting in the loss of either their own voice in the partnership or a loss of the connection with their partner. The anger functions as a way to help the attachment system maintain closeness or proximity to a loved one as the threat detection system evaluates the danger of losing the connection.[1] Most often, this behavior does not end up in provoking the intended outcome of bringing their partner closer.

An unfortunate consequence of this movement toward an attachment figure out of anger is that it can also activate the other partner's threat detection system. Most of the time, their brain is not able to detect their partner's desperate plea to connect and avoid a loss. Their threat detection system hears a change in the prosody of the voice:[3] louder, more high pitched tones and words that cut like daggers as they go behind their wall to protect themselves from the attack. Many of my clients in the withdrawing position describe feeling chiseled at by their partners. They go behind the safety of their walls because they aren't feeling accepted or valued either. They are feeling attacked and criticized, triggering their need to take emotional shelter. The more they go behind their wall to protect themselves from attack, the more their partner fears the loss of the connection and continues to fight to break through the wall. Both partners are in a lose-lose situation here.

Some withdrawers also use their anger as a protector. They start to get verbally hostile to keep people from emotionally coming close to them, where it doesn't feel emotionally safe. Clients may also get hostile as a protective stance to allow them to avoid their emotions and vulnerability. It's a sense of "I don't want to go here, I don't want you to make me go here, please get back and go away, so I don't have to." This can be extremely triggering for therapists when they do sense underlying pain, and come up against the client's defenses every time they try to get close to, understand, or make sense of the client's reactivity.

The function of hostility

I find hostile anger the most triggering as it tends to be the most self-protective, and ends up leaving others feeling completely helpless and hopeless as to how to break through the walls and reach the person in pain underneath. The function of hostile anger highlights the nature of angry behavior, as it is also designed to warn approaching aggressors to stop their attacks and threatening behavior or to deter them from coming close.

Oftentimes what I see happen between couples is the withdrawing partner might throw verbal grenades at their partner as they attempt to flee from the conversation, sometimes even the room. Think of it this way; it's like a soldier trying to take refuge in a cave, but must thwart the oncoming approach of an enemy. If they can throw a grenade at the enemy, they might have a chance of deterring the enemy from continuing to advance. Most of the time, this also doesn't have the desired effect, because grenades, by design, tend to blow things up and hurt people. Usually, it pours more gas on the fire rather than extinguishing it because both pursuing and withdrawing positions are responding to a threat, and the anger functions differently for each person. If we fail to see that anger is a response to threat and a sign of pain, then it can be hard to have empathy for an angry person and be able to lean into their anger to understand the message of their anger.

So when we see reactive behavior, it's important to realize this is a clue of a perceived threat. Remember, when the brain detects possible disconnection from others, it is encoded as a threat. Our survival instincts mobilize us into reactivity behavior for the benefit of our survival. Anger is a sign of pain or fear.[1] Anger as an emotion is a reaction to detected danger or threat, even though angry behavior sometimes gets displayed in a way that communicates threat or danger to others. Anger itself is not bad, actually, it's such an important emotion. If we can learn to distinguish the difference between anger as an emotion and angry behavior, then we can offer a path toward leaning into anger, understanding what it's fighting for, and having more flexibility and control over how the anger gets expressed, ideally in a way that doesn't pose a threat to others.

An example of this might be when feeling hurt or betrayed by another, to express the anger as an honest representation of one's internal experience. Such as, "I am so angry, the message I just got is that what I have to say is not important and I really want to know my voice is important to you." Notice the language is self-directed, not blaming or focusing outward on someone else, and directly expressing feelings of anger. This is just one of many ways of expressing anger in a different way that is authentic and direct to one's internal reality.

After reading the example above, what ways can you come up with to express your anger differently?

Violence in relationships

When violence occurs in the relationships of clients we treat, it can trigger our natural sense of justice, and activate our protective instincts to protect the person we feel is being harmed. It's easy to have empathy for someone who is being hurt. It's not as easy to have empathy for someone who is doing the hurting. Yet, if we can't find a path to having empathy for those clients too, how will they ever truly get the help they need?

Having empathy for those that commit violence in relationships is an area where therapists definitely can struggle. While having internal feelings about the violence is inevitable, being able to stay out of judgment and have empathy for both partners will help create an avenue for which change can occur. Therapists may get caught judging the violent behavior, and labeling the violent partner as an abuser, and start directing the other partner to leave the relationship. While it's important to create safety in session and in relationships, this judgment does not offer a safe path forward where the violence can be explored and understood, and the couple can heal their relationship.

It's a natural instinct to want to point out and blame the person who's committing violent behavior. But remember, it's unethical for us to judge, and it keeps us out of empathy. We don't need to decide who's the bad guy or judge the behavior as hurtful because the distress in the relationship does that for us. If we tune in to the distress, it speaks for itself. When we can remember this, it's easier to avoid judgment and stick to helping the people in pain.

Clients have a hard time disclosing violence because many of them are ashamed of their behavior and are afraid of judgment. If the client cannot come to therapy and not be judged for the parts they aren't proud of, what chance do they have to really find healing and change? Their shame comes from behaving in ways that are contrary to who or how they want to be. They may act out using violence even though they aren't normally violent people; the behavior is against their normal character. People do not normally act out with violence when they feel in control of themselves and the situation. Everyone is capable of losing it, snapping, and doing something out of character from a place of extreme anger.[5]

This type of violence is known as situational couple violence (SCV),[6] and is not the same as "domestic violence," or "intimate terrorism"[7] in which violence is unidirectional and used to control and isolate another.[5,6] Research discusses that situational couple violence, which is bidirectional, meaning both partners may participate in the violent behavior, is one of the most commonly occurring types of violence therapists will come across in therapy.[5,6,7]

It's important to distinguish that acting out in violence does not make someone an abuser or abusive. This word gets so easily tossed around when it really isn't appropriate for the situation or behavior. The word "abuse" has been very "abused." According to the dictionary definition, abuse simply means an improper treatment or usage. According to that definition, every single person alive has probably been guilty of abuse at some point. The point is not to say that we shouldn't call abuse abuse, but the term needs to stop being so liberally applied to every behavior which is hurtful. Violence and abuse are different, but regardless of which applies, a person committing either still needs our help if they are to change. If we approach these reactive behaviors with judgment, we won't be in a good position to help create that change.

All too often therapists dismiss the person committing the violence as an abuser, as if they don't have legitimate pain or distress that needs to be addressed and understood. They may not be comfortable directly dealing with it, and therefore don't lean in emotionally and listen to the pain being communicated by the behavior. Usually by the time violence has entered into the equation, the personal committing violence has already tried to communicate in other ways. Violence is the communication of last resort, of utter hopelessness and desperation, when it seems as though it is the only way to get the message across as all other communication has been unsuccessful. Most people who commit violence will admit the behavior is not ideal. It's not what they wanted either. Feeling pushed into a corner without options; this is where control is lost or surrendered. Most clients will tell you if they felt like they had control in those moments, they would do something different.

There is a reason the violence is happening,[5] and therapists need to be able to have these direct conversations together with their couples in session. This cannot be done without being able to have relentless empathy, even for the one committing the violence. Again, this is not saying to validate violent behavior, only to validate the pain and emotion underneath the violent behavior.

Research has already linked violence in adult attachment relationships with insecure attachment. In securely attached couples, partners are able to help co-regulate emotions, offer soothing, and de-escalate together. In insecurely attached couples with SCV, the emotions connected to their attachment strategies create escalating patterns. It is the attachment frame that allows us to maintain a stance of relentless empathy for couples engaged in these patterns, and the partners engaging in these behaviors. Through that frame, it is easier for the therapist to explore and gain insight into the relationship dynamics that drive SCV. The more we can stay in a positive and safe alliance with each partner in SCV, the more we are able to help clients into safer territory and more effective behavior.

It's an old school frame of reference to say that the presence of violence contra-indicates couples therapy.[5] This is no longer the case. Research also shows that couples therapy can help reduce the risk of violence with SCV. With these couples, the therapist will have to do thorough, ongoing assessment of the couple as to the type of violence and the context and function of it. Clients cannot be directed into intentional emotional vulnerability until the violent behavior has stopped. However, if therapists can create safety in session, and the couple has mutually agreed upon coming to therapy, it is reasonable to work with the couple and directly address the violence as part of understanding their cycle of escalation. The same strategies for understanding anger can be used to unpack and understand violence in relationships as violence is an extreme expression of anger.

Leaning into anger

One of the worst things you can say to someone who's angry is "calm down." This says to their nervous system, "I can't deal with you" or "just get over it." It feels very dismissive of a person's very real visceral reality, which understandably would arouse more anger.

Trying to offer logical solutions to someone who's angry also doesn't match their experience. Logic is a function of the frontal cortex, and emotion is a function of the limbic system that instinctively directs us to our safety. The frontal cortex cannot talk the limbic system out of its pain. Cognition is impotent with unprocessed pain and fear. Clients will often say, "logically I know this, but emotionally, I still feel this way." This is why it's vital to work with people on the level of their emotional experiencing. It is the limbic system that needs to have the change experience to feel safe again, not just the frontal cortex. The limbic system needs to be able to revise a previously dangerous narrative or cue as safe.

When we can recognize that anger is pain or fear, it can be easier to tolerate their anger and stay in a window of empathy and tolerance. The more we can tolerate the heat of anger, the more we can help open up and make some space to understand what their anger is about. In this way, we're like emotional firefighters. We have to be able to run into the fire of heated emotions, and we have to tolerate very hot emotional spaces in order to help people and extinguish the anger. Relentless empathy helps us to bravely enter the fiery space of emotion without getting burned up. It can help us tolerate the heat without going on the defensive ourselves. Their anger or hostility, even when directed at us, is not a sign that we're bad at our jobs. It's a call for help.

When clients turn to us and start poking at us, attacking our age, marital status, whether or not we have kids, or the number of years in practice, they are actually asking, "Can you really help me?" They need reassurance. They need to know that we can and will show up for them in this painful place and help them. They need to know they will be responded to empathically and that they won't be abandoned.

Before I really understood emotion, the function of emotion, and the important information contained in emotional signals, I would get dysregulated in these moments, which would hijack my presence into self-protection and I would end up not fully leaning into these vital moments where the client needed me the most. Since anger is pain, when the client gets angry, it means I've touched a nerve, something they feel very deeply and arouses their nervous system and brings up their defenses. I've learned through this that I don't need to be afraid of the client's anger. That client's anger is like striking gold. There's a lot of rich information in their emotional signals if we have the courage to stay in the heat with them long enough to find out what it is. When I learned to see my clients' anger as pain and not a criticism of me or rejection, I was able to remain calm and stay in the fire of emotion with them where they needed me most.

When I've had angry spouses get activated in session and start yelling at their partner and blaming them, I learned not to be afraid to wedge myself between their attacks (emotionally, though sometimes I've had to physically sit between angry partners to interrupt hostility) and really lean in and get curious about their anger. I have realized that when anger comes alive in my session, that person is giving me valuable insight into their experience. They're telling me they're in pain, and/or they're afraid, and they need me to show up for them. Without being able to recognize anger as pain, I wouldn't be able to have empathy every time someone gets really angry in session.

It is hard when clients start to yell and maybe stand up and get real big (also a sign of feeling threatened) and storm out. In my early days of this, I learned how important it was to call the client and do a repair and let them know, "I'm sorry you didn't feel heard right there, I'd really like to understand your anger if you're willing to help me get it." Most of the time, this has been really powerful and transformative for the client's anger. Once we meet anger where it is, it will shift and get calmer. It's not always instantaneous as the body also has to come down from the adrenaline rush and rapid heartbeat. But the more you can get curious about the message of their anger, the more they'll feel heard and understood, and their anger won't feel the need to fight as hard.

Many therapists struggle to lean into anger because they're afraid validating someone's angry emotions (not behavior) means the anger will get bigger. Angry behavior can feel very scary, and can tip us out of our own window of tolerance. Leaning into anger doesn't make it bigger; it actually has the opposite effect. When you meet anger where it is, it will shift and start to calm. The function of their anger is to help what's underneath get heard. When you clearly make explicit the emotional attachment message of their anger, they won't need to fight so hard anymore to get heard.

What also becomes hard about leaning into anger, even when you do have empathy for it, is coming up against the client's highly advanced defense system. I have some clients that are so well defended and seem to outmaneuver me whenever I get close, while simultaneously getting angry every time I get close. I've learned that the more highly defended the person is, the more their previous experience(s) has taught them the need for those defenses. I think people are easily fooled by angry reactivity and don't recognize that the more easily angered a person is, the more sensitive they actually are. These clients have developed elaborate defensive strategies to protect the rawness that exists underneath. It can show up in session when exploring their anger leads to frequent upsets, defensiveness, and reactivity.

I once had a client that was so clearly angry in session with his wife, but as I reflected his anger, he seemed to have a very visceral response to my even using the word anger, and would reject any notion that he was angry (even though on the outside it was so clear). It seemed no matter which emotional or mental doorway I tried to reach the client through, I would be met with their blocks and defenses. It was so hard to break through. And as a pursuer myself, my tendency in the past has been to try to break down walls when they are put up, not realizing the function of the wall for the person on the other side. This client was like a live wire in session, and every attempt to validate and reflect his behavior or experience would spark a reaction, and he would push away with hostility. I had to take a deep breath and step back.

What I had to learn about these types of angry clients is that this angry defensiveness is symptomatic of feeling *constant* threat.[1] Somehow, even my use of the word anger was a threat. So I had to work really hard to stay in my window of tolerance and lean into the threat. It seemed so clear that he cared about his wife and that every time he upset her, it was intolerable to him. He would get so defensive and say, "so I'm the jerk here, I'm the bad guy." (This is a very common response I hear in angry clients.)

As he started to feel like the bad guy, he didn't realize his angry rejections of his wife's feelings began reinforcing in her the exact feeling he was wanting to extinguish. Talk about a bind! He wasn't a jerk, nor was he a bad guy. He was in pain. And I had to get curious as to why being seen as angry was such a threat to him. I had to take a risk and say out loud,

> I notice whenever I use the word angry to describe the emotion that comes across on the outside, that that triggers a strong response for you. Something about being angry really does not sit well for you, can you help me understand that?

What the client was saying was that for him, being seen as angry reinforced the view of himself that he was attempting to reject: the view that being the bad guy—just being angry meant, for him, that he was the bad guy. Even though he was clearly reacting with anger, the function of rejecting both of these things was to protect himself from being the bad guy. Because in his attachment experience, being the bad guy meant he wasn't worthy of love or care. He also desperately wanted and needed someone to see him as fighting for his marriage and loving his partner.

This client really needed to be seen as the good guy, even though his behavior was reactive and hurtful. Being able to make sense of this and talk about how I struggled to get through his defenses to get close to his emotional pain at least opened up some emotional space to have a different conversation. He didn't want me close to his pain as long as he thought I was going to see him as the bad guy. His evasive, defensive, and hostile responses served a protective function. And I had to validate that. I wouldn't have been able to stay long enough in the heat of his hostile defenses had I not been able to have relentless empathy for him.

Pain demands to be felt, and anger demands to be heard. We tend to think that because someone is angry and being hurtful that they don't care or don't need care. Rather, they are more like a wounded animal; they lash out and hurt because they are hurting and need care. They can also build walls with their anger, to hide behind when they're in pain. The irony is that those that don't understand anger give the least amount of empathy to someone who's angry, when empathy is the exact thing that's needed to corrode the anger.

And remember, validating a client's angry emotions doesn't mean we're validating their angry outbursts, like in the 1970s and 1980s where it was believed to be cathartic to have clients use foam bats or punch punching bags to express and vent their anger.[8] Researchers actually found in those cases that punching something while angry does not decrease anger or feelings of aggression, and sometimes can actually make it worse.[8]

We can't tear down someone's walls or defenses for them. The more we try, the more their survival instincts will dig in and hang onto those defenses. What we're trying to do is create enough safety that the client no longer needs their walls or their defenses to feel safe. When we can do this, the client will eventually come to the point where they realize on their own that their walls or defenses are no longer serving them, but are a barrier to them getting what they need and want.

None of this would be possible without being able to have relentless empathy for angry people. It's easier to have empathy for softer, less threatening emotional reactivity, but anger needs relentless empathy too. I've found that the more pain there is, the deeper the fear, the deeper the wound, the more the anger. People may say very hurtful things when they're angry, or act in ways that feel big and scary. They need empathy too. The more we can recognize the call for help, the more our relentless empathy will give us the courage to lean in and show up for their anger, which is exactly what the anger needs.

Leaning in will help your client feel understood, and will open up more emotional space for you to work on finding alternative ways to help the client be successful in getting themselves heard and understood. In couples therapy, it can also be very powerful in modeling for their partner how to show up and handle their angry spouse. The most powerful thing you can do for someone who's angry, is show up for them, show relentless empathy, which will allow you to lean in and get curious and really listen for the message of their anger.

Practice activity: Leaning into your own anger

Therapists aren't immune to feeling hurt, angry, or disconnected with their partners or people they care about. One of the ways I learned how to master the skill of leaning into anger was by putting these principles at work on myself. How much safer could it be to tolerate someone's anger than to tolerate my own? It also allowed me to step into the shoes of someone who's angry and see if showing up in that space would work, and in fact, it did.

I had a conflict with a mentor that left me feeling quite angry and reactive. Mentors, especially our first, can feel almost like professional parents; their opinion and approval means something to us. So, of course, conflict with a mentor can be just as hard as conflict with a loved one. When this happened, all I wanted to do was vent and poke at my mentor (only privately in my head because I knew doing this wouldn't help the relationship). I was so angry, and the situation felt so unfair. I could feel the anger in the pit of my stomach; my head felt like it was on fire. I was livid. At that moment, I put on my EFT hat and practiced what I do with clients. I showed up for my own anger.

I leaned inward and I asked myself, "What is this anger all about? What is the important message that my anger is trying to get heard? If my anger could have a clear voice, what would it want to be known?" I could hear myself answer with, "I feel so unseen for my hard work, and feel unimportant to my mentor, whose professional validation does mean something to me." As this message now became clear, I could actually feel my blood pressure start to come down. I felt a literal shift inside my body. I became much more in touch with the sadness and hurt that lay just underneath the anger. My anger began shifting, and I became calm again. I could feel that tension in the pit in my stomach go away. This exercise also helped me come to clarity about what I wanted to share with my mentor without coming across as attacking or threatening myself. The strategy had worked!

Most of the time, when I do this with clients, I can see the same visceral response to being heard, seen, and understood as well. I've learned to lean in and say something like, "this anger is helping me know there's something really important that needs to be understood, and I'd really like to know more about what that is." Many clients have even thanked me for helping them make sense of their own anger by doing this. After making sense of the client's anger, we were able to map out their moves in their dance of disconnection when they get angry and establish whether or not that move was an effective strategy or not.

Most clients also then begin to be able to tolerate hearing that their strategies of poking, attacking, or criticizing their partner aren't an effective way of getting their partner to show up for them, to love them, or give them the support they were needing. Once a client feels heard and understood, we are able to collaboratively work together on creating new, more healthy and effective strategies for being heard by their partners or loved ones, and for getting their needs met.

The success of these strategies has really validated and reinforced the powerful impact relentless empathy can have in dealing with and responding to anger. We need to remember that anger is pain or fear, and that it needs us to emotionally come close, listen to it, and make very clear and explicit the message of anger and what its function is. Because of relentless empathy, we no longer need to be afraid of anger. We can start to see angry people as hurting people longing to be understood and be cared for, and we can show up for them differently.

Self of the therapist window of tolerance exercise

A. The following are a few questions to ask yourself about your own views of anger:

1. How do I feel about other people's anger? About my own anger?
2. What do I notice I do when people around me get angry? What do I do when anger is directed toward me? Is it different when the anger is coming from a client or from a loved one?
3. How do I currently make meaning out of people's anger?
4. Am I willing and able to lean into people's anger with relentless empathy and curiosity?
5. If not, what do I need to do to be willing and able to lean into people's anger with relentless empathy and curiosity? (For example: Get supervision, do some personal work in your own therapy around the emotion of anger)

B. The following exercise is a personal reflection exercise that will help you explore and understand your own window of tolerance (WOT) for working with emotions. The following questions ask about your own emotional comfort zone:

1. When I'm with a client, or listening to someone (like a friend/colleague/loved one), the emotion that most likely triggers/activates me and pushes me out of my WOT is (for example: Fear? Shame? Anger? Sadness? Hurt? Silence?):
2. When this happens, the *thought* I have (what I say to myself) is:
3. When I have this thought or say this to myself, what is the emotion I have that comes along with this?
4. What do I *do* when this happens? When I feel that I am outside of my WOT? (For example: I push harder or demand. I teach or explain. I go into my head and go silent.)
5. When facing this place and the emotions that come along with it, my *fear* is (what do I imagine is the worst thing that could happen if I stay with the other person's emotions?):
6. What do I need in these moments, to stay grounded while I am working on expanding my WOT by staying with my deeper emotions or the emotions of others?

Notes

1 Mikulincer, M., & Shaver, P. R. (2011). Attachment, anger, and aggression. In P. R. Shaver & M. Mikulincer (Eds.), *Herzilya series on personality and social psychology. Human aggression and violence: Causes, manifestations, and consequences* (pp. 241–257). Washington, DC: American Psychological Association.
2 Shaver, P., Schwartz, J., Kirson, D., & O'Connor, C. (1987), Emotion knowledge: Further exploration of a prototype approach. *Journal of Personality and Social Psychology*, 52: 1061–1086.
3 Porges, S. W. (2007). The polyvagal perspective. *Biological Psychology*, 74(2): 116–143.
4 SAMHSA. (2018). First Responders: Behavioral Health Concerns, Emergency Response, and Trauma.
5 Johnson, M. P., & Leone, J. M. (2005). The differential effects of intimate terrorism and situational couple violence: Findings from the National Violence Against Women Survey. *Journal of Family Issues*, 26: 322–349.
6 Treating violence in couples therapy. Migerode, L., & Slootmaeckers, J. (2018). Fighting for connection: Patterns of intimate partner violence. *Journal of Couples & Relationship Therapy*, 17(4): 294–312.

7 Durfee, A. (2011). Intimate terrorism and situational couple violence. *Gender and Society, 25*(4): 522–524. Retrieved from www.jstor.org/stable/23044209
8 Busham, B. J. (2016). Does venting anger feed or extinguish the flame? Catharsis, rumination, distraction, anger, and aggressive responding. *Personality and Social Psychology Bulletin, 28*(6): 724–731.

Chapter 7

Relentless empathy for difficult people in your life

Personal and professional applications for everyday life

> The highest form of knowledge is Empathy.
> George Eliot, Victorian Novelist

We are relational beings hardwired for connection. We, as human beings, never stop looking for signs of safety and connection with others.[1] We are never not in relationships with other humans, though the type of interaction and relationship may define the type of emotional investment or risk involved in maintaining the connection. Just because we leave our office or the therapy room doesn't mean that we stop needing to feel emotionally safe in the connections we have or desire to have in our personal lives. We need to remember that the same skills and principles we use to have relentless empathy at work can also be used to help us relate to all human interactions and create a connection with others in our own lives as well as the outside world. These principles should never leave us.

This is especially important to remember because the values we ascribe to as therapists and clinicians, the things we work on with our clients, should not change just because we've left our office. As penned by George Eliot above, empathy *is* our highest form of knowledge and our knowledge and values as therapists need to be embodied in us as human beings in general. Remembering that being patient with someone's reactive anger, for example, doesn't stop just because we're in the grocery store, posting on Facebook, or in our therapist chairs seeing clients. This is what makes us authentic, genuine, and ethically congruent. Otherwise, as hard as it may be to say, we are frauds.

It has been very surprising to me that some clinicians, mentors, supervisors, leaders, seem to forget this as they interact with us in the outside world. In EFT, we learn to master the art of bringing two truths together and creating connection.[1] This is a challenging aspect of working with couples in therapy. It can still generally be very challenging when it comes to interacting with other humans in the world, especially ones whose personal views or behaviors are very different from our own. Sometimes these differences even feel threatening.

Becoming an EFT therapist was life-changing for me. Most therapists are pretty good at empathy, but *relentless* empathy is a whole new level and a whole new skill. EFT teaches us how to harness the power of relentless empathy to build better connections with other people,[1] while attachment science teaches us how to see and understand human beings differently, more empathically. Understanding that we are all attachment-driven beings and that we are hardwired to look for signs of safety from others was revolutionary in helping me empathize with clients and challenging people in my personal life. Our emotions help give us vital clues about our experiences in the world, and our automatic ability to make meaning helps us use those emotional clues to tell our brain whether something around us is meant for our harm or our benefit.

It's important to remember that when we see someone out in the real world get angry or reactive, the same principles apply. Their brain is kicked into survival mode, registering a possible attachment threat, and mobilizing them into fight or flight to help them emotionally survive. If we can remember this, it's a lot easier to stay in a frame of relentless empathy for them, and then it's a bit easier to start to see underneath the surface of their reactive behavior to the fears and longings in their heart. This can become more challenging when we're the one experiencing the threat. Maybe someone we care about, love, respect, or look up to is saying or doing something that doesn't feel very safe or loving. Applying these principles to ourselves in the face of threat, understanding what's at play, and approaching these people can feel really daunting. Learning how to apply these principles to yourself, and then using that to have relentless empathy for the other person, can help us approach having a challenging conversation without coming out with our guns blazing (metaphorically speaking that is).

For example, when I'm reading a political post by a mentor on Facebook, making blanket statements about people who do not agree with their stance, making assumptions about the core of who I am, it can be hard to stand forward and say, "this doesn't feel safe, is there another way here?" Or when a supervisor gets critical with us and seems to abandon all cues of safety, the hardest thing to do is speak up and say something in a way that doesn't return the emotional threat.

When I remembered that attachment has given me a very clear and explicit roadmap to understanding human behavior and why people act and react the way that they do, and combine that with my skills and training as an EFT therapist, I was able to master a better approach to solving problems and disconnection with other people.

Authority figures need safety too

Sometimes we can fail to show empathy to authority figures because we look up to them and assume they have it made or have it all together. When people have careers or promotions we want, we can be tempted to believe it came without struggle, and we forget that even our leaders are human too. We look to them for safety, acceptance, and approval, and don't often recognize they need it from us as well.

I regularly volunteer to help out at special training events for new clinicians. At one particular event, I was working with a mentor with whom I have a tremendous amount of respect for. This mentor administered much of my formal training as a therapist and helped me become a mastery level EFT clinician. At one point, I heard my mentor discussing and sharing some interesting points on attachment. Usually, experienced volunteers are welcome to contribute comments and share some of their knowledge at appropriate times during these events.

During the discussion on attachment, while a lot of people were raising their hands, I raised my hand and contributed a comment that felt like icing on the cake. Immediately after I shared my comment, my mentor shot me the laser death look. It was cold; it was piercing, it cut deep. I could feel it in my gut, which started to feel like my insides were twisting up. And the worst part was, I was sure others had seen the look I was given. I felt humiliated. I felt hurt.

Was I wrong? Had I done something wrong? Had I said something completely incorrect? I didn't think so, as I replayed my comment in my head to check it for factual accuracy. It was, in fact, something I had heard my mentor say several times before. So it couldn't have been that. I quietly sneaked out of the back of the room and went outside for some air. I was feeling overwhelmed with hurt and humiliation, which was now starting to turn into anger for having received what felt like condemnation in front of a group of peers I was soon going to be in charge of leading. I thought, "how could they do this to me?" If I was wrong, why couldn't my mentor have saved their death stare from piercing me in front of the group and instead shared their thoughts with me privately?

I walked around to the side of the building to some benches where I could have some privacy under the shade of a nearby tree. I took a deep breath. What had just happened? I felt awful. I felt completely wronged. I owned and acknowledged my feelings and that it felt really bad to receive such a look in a public forum. This was the message of my anger and hurt. This, at least, helped me calm my anger and allowed me to return to the training calm and collected for the time being. But make no mistake, I was still chewing on this inside.

It wasn't until I was driving home from the event later that day, processing over the phone with a trusted close confidant (also a therapist) that I was able to make sense of my mentor's behavior. As I was talking about what had happened, I realized that in order to not butt heads with my mentor, in order to preserve the relationship, I needed to put on my EFT hat and see this through the same lens at which I would if it were a couple I was seeing. I remembered what attachment had taught me about human behavior and that if I wanted to preserve the relationship, I needed to step into my mentor's shoes and try to see it from their perspective. The ability to do this is a hallmark trait of being able to empathize with someone.

I tend to be very outspoken and outgoing. This means sometimes I can offer unsolicited comments that aren't always well received, even though it comes from a loving place of excitement and care. I had to put myself on the other side and remember that on the outside, not everyone can automatically detect intention. I had to remember that even well-intentioned people can step on toes too.

So I thought about it from my mentor's perspective. What if I had been hired to present at a conference or an event and someone who held a position that technically ranked below mine kept sharing their two cents? How would I feel about that? People get reactive in the presence of a threat. Is there a way that my unsolicited comments could have registered to my mentor as a threat? At that moment, the lightbulb came on. In their position, I would probably think, "does this person think I'm stupid or that they know better than I?" It was then that I was able to recognize that my comment could have come off to my mentor like I thought they didn't know what they were talking about and that I knew better.

I immediately felt empathy once again. I knew that I would feel awful in their position. What also dawned on me is that the whole time, while I, a new leader in our profession, was looking for cues of safety and acceptance by my mentor, my mentor was also looking for signs of safety from me. I had neglected to see the humanness of my mentor and that just because they were in a position of authority over me, didn't mean they didn't still need safety and acceptance just as much as I did. I felt a calmness come over me as the knot in my gut disappeared. Just because leaders seem like they have it made, doesn't mean they don't still need acceptance too. They need acceptance from me just as much as I need it from them.

I ended up meeting my mentor for dinner, and I was able to bring up what had happened previously that day. I'll admit it was hard to bring up the conversation. How do you approach your boss and say, "I didn't feel safe with you today, can we talk about it?" But I took a risk and owned my part while I also let my mentor know that while I had felt very hurt to receive such a cold look, the look hurt because my mentor mattered to me. Their respect and opinion about me as a leader mattered to me. I also told my mentor that by using my EFT training to work through this, I realized that my mentor also needed acceptance and safety from me and that my comment could have come across as "I know better than you." My mentor was impressed and thanked me for having the courage to have the conversation. I also received an apology and a deep recognition by my mentor that leaders aren't exempt from humanness and needing acceptance.

It felt really good to have the repair with my mentor. What felt even better was the shared understanding that we are all human, no matter what job or title we may hold. We all long for acceptance from others.

Using relentless empathy in the workplace

I once had a friend, I'll call her Jenny, whose new boss, I'll call him Zahr, was proving to be a royal difficulty for them. Zahr had recently been recruited from overseas and didn't speak the language well. He was brought in under the belief that he would be among senior leadership, a position which he had held in his own country for over a decade, and instead was given a lower position and was now a gofer for the senior leadership team. He was made supervisor over a department he never agreed to oversee. To make matters worse, five months after Zahr was hired, the company announced a reorganization, which meant every employee was going to be evaluated and possibly laid off.

Zahr would often act very condescending and dismissive of my friend's input on team projects. He also had very little experience on the special projects team he was now in charge of, and often gave Jenny a very hard time about things she was extremely knowledgeable about. When Jenny did excellent work, Zahr often would take credit for the accomplishments. He was also somewhat of a loner at work and didn't talk much unless he had to. Jenny had a hard time working with him and started to really hate her job. She grew angry and irritated that he seemed to be squashing her contributions and taking credit for her accomplishments.

As we discussed Zahr further, I saw that Jenny was looking for ways to create change in this challenging work dynamic. I challenged Jenny to walk in Zahr's shoes. This man was brought over from a foreign country and more or less deceived by the company CEO as to what he would be coming on board to do. He relocated his family halfway around the world to a strange place and a new culture, where feeling accepted by others has proven to be quite difficult. He was isolated, he was alone, and once the reorganization was announced, he was panicked as to the fate of his job. He was, in many ways, set up to fail. That didn't make his behavior okay. Still, it helped Jenny better understand his motives and how he was desperately trying to prove his value and be seen as a valuable asset by his own leadership team, whom he was originally supposed to be a part of.

Once we were able to understand how difficult of a spot Zahr was in, it was a lot easier to start having empathy for him. Jenny reflected that she no longer disliked Zahr, but actually started to feel empathy for him, which led her to feel compassion for Zahr.

She began finding ways to try to help him feel seen and valued for his own skills, not just by taking credit for Jenny's accomplishments. As this started to happen, Jenny noticed he had started to soften at work, and the environment felt much less tense. Zahr was even able to open up to Jenny and share how rough it had been for him in this transition. He expressed how lost he had felt and how no one had offered him an olive branch of acceptance until Jenny. This fostered a whole new working relationship between them, and even though he was eventually let go during the reorganization, Jenny was able to connect him with some contacts, and he was able to get a position with another company, better suited to his skills and experience.

Months later, he called Jenny to thank her for her help and reported that he was flourishing in his new company, but that he would have never had the courage or confidence without Jenny's support and acceptance. Jenny thanked me for helping her learn how to have relentless empathy for her colleague and said it had continued to have a profound ripple effect on all of her work relationships, as she was also in a leadership position.

Relentless empathy on the world's stage

Facebook has allowed us to bridge the gaps in geography and build connections over a long distance. While I can't say Facebook is all positive, I can say that it is increasingly used by colleagues, friends, and families today. It was on Facebook that a personal interaction with a colleague was changed because of the ways in which EFT taught us how to have relentless empathy for others.

Our political climate today seems to relish in extreme polarities. I wish this wasn't the case, but it seems even taking a stance in the middle of the road seems to upset someone on one side or the other, and immediately someone gets reactive. What's really hard is when I have colleagues with whom I have to interact with professionally and to whom I sometimes refer clients, who seem to forget when they make political statements on Facebook, that just because we are using a personal forum, that we are still looking for signs of emotional safety. I'd say this point is most poignantly relevant today. If more people could approach problems via connection like my colleague and I did on Facebook, the world would be a much more connected place.

The reason I mention politics is that it has become the source of frequent posts by family, friends, and yes, many fellow clinicians with whom I am acquainted with on Facebook. I've noticed it quickly gets heated, and people can quickly get ugly. It especially disheartens me when I see trained clinicians participate in the bullying of others because they don't agree. I am friends with several of my colleagues and mentors, many of whom I couldn't be more diametrically opposite of politically. I try to refrain from commenting on political posts now because whenever I try to see the other side of the argument, I get called names, and basically ganged up on by strangers from both sides, though each is heavily preaching tolerance!

But it was actually such a post that started out heated and ended in creating a deeper connection between myself and a colleague because we were able to use our EFT skills to have relentless empathy for each other. This post started with something I shared from a friend that was a link to an interesting article on an issue that had religious and political implications. The article wasn't even taking a stance on an issue, but provided two sides of an argument. So I did not expect the vitriol that was about to ensue on my Facebook post. Little had I realized that in sharing the article as an interesting read, I had just lit a match and set off an explosion of opinions.

One of my colleagues, I'll call him Kevin, who lives on the east coast of the US, ended up getting involved in my post. Kevin and I had interacted on several occasions, had done some social media interviews together, and had a positive working alliance, but didn't really know each other personally that well. During the course of observing people's comments, I found that many others were making hurtful assumptions about people of particular religious views, which felt judgmental and unfair.

As things progressed, both Kevin and I started to interject and began to feel our amygdala's firing up (the survival part of the brain that detects threat) as we exchanged opinions. What followed was relationship-changing. Both of us were able to use our skills as therapists to speak more about the emotional process that was starting to unfold between us. Our comments began saying things like, "my amygdala is firing off, are you saying XYZ?" And as we did this, we were able to recognize the threat each other was feeling, and change our comments to go in a different direction that created more safety. What we ended up creating was a deeper understanding of each other that blossomed into a beautiful friendship. It was really wonderful how we were able to recognize the threat and mobilize to create safety and connection.

As our comments began changing, and we started showing empathy for each other, others on the post started to take notice. Their comments started to change and many even remarked on how nice it was to see two people with different perspectives come together around our humanity. It was exciting to have others witness the ability to create a connection despite having different views.

Moreover, my friend Kevin and I began messaging each other outside of the post, discussing what personal experiences had informed our perspectives. It was a delightful exchange because Kevin and I learned so much about each other as people. We began sharing our experiences of being bullied during our school years, and we were able to offer acceptance and empathy for each other. We both ended up discovering that we actually had a lot of experiences and views in common. Kevin and I have such an incredible friendship now; something that wouldn't have happened had we not been able to practice relentless empathy with each other.

It felt so rewarding to go from two people with polar opposite views, to being able to use our understanding of attachment and our training as EFT therapists to work through a heated discussion. To be able to use relentless empathy to build a beautiful friendship. This whole experience has allowed us to find a surprising friendship where we least expected it.

Also, having had this exchange on Facebook set an example for others to follow. This helps bring the skills of relentless empathy to the world stage in a way that can help build connections and friendships where otherwise they wouldn't exist. If we can harness the skills of relentless empathy where we previously might have seen a possible threat or enemy, we can create a connection and possibly make a new friend. At the risk of sounding trite, if we could all learn to have relentless empathy for others, we could reshape disconnected relationships around the world. Now that would be something!

Directions for relentless empathy

I am thankful for each of these experiences that I mentioned in this chapter. Each of them taught me something different, but each of them resulted in being able to harness the power of relentless empathy to approach things from a different angle. With *relentless empathy* in my heart and attachment in my vision, I was able to shape relationships with other people in difficult situations, which resulted in deeper connections that I wouldn't have otherwise been able to have. I enjoy having relationships with diverse people who can think differently than I do. How else will I learn to grow and evolve and be grounded if I can't see things from all sides?

And while I enjoy relationships like this, it also presents some difficulties and challenges at times. Sometimes it's uncomfortable, and perhaps a bit terrifying, to have challenging conversations with someone you care about, even professionally, because you don't always know how it's going to be received. But I do know that when I've been able to maintain a heart of relentless empathy, the other person was able to tolerate the difficult conversation and work through it with me. This is probably because our emotions shape our behavior. When we feel empathy, we are less likely to be reactive, angry, critical or judgmental ... we become safe even though we might be bringing up a sensitive or difficult conversation.

On the world's stage, we may be in situations where we may have the authority or capacity to remediate a problem. However, when confronted by a difficult person or customer, who pounds us with anger or criticism, it can be challenging to maintain empathy, which may make us less likely to want to help that person or fix the problematic situation.

One of the key skills for having a conversation with a challenging or difficult person is to be able to tolerate someone else's pain. Many people now have become so pain averse that when they see another in pain (especially when it looks like anger), they turn away from the pain, especially if we feel they have targeted us with their pain. They may turn away from the pain by dismissing the other person's reality, telling them they're irrational, or using logical facts to tell them why they're wrong. We can better tolerate someone else's pain by again remembering they're sharing or directing their pain toward us as a plea for help. Though we may not have the ability to fix the situation, we can show care through empathy and understanding, and help facilitate better options for them in their pain. This gives us greater flexibility to stay in the conversation with that person without feeling drained or weighed down by it, and guide the interaction in a way that results in greater success.

Having relentless empathy does not mean allowing other people to be hurtful. It means being able to understand what's at work in human behavior when people do behave in hurtful ways, and being open to making space for more than one side of the story without it feeling like a threat. It means being able to see both sides, while still honoring your own voice and value. Doing this while being able to share your feelings in a way that doesn't provoke a sense of threat in the other party. It means being able to tolerate when people are difficult, seeing below the surface of their reactivity to their humanity, and keeping humanity in focus as we work through the challenges to get what every person needs in the end: love, acceptance, belonging, and emotional safety. None of these would be possible without relentless empathy.

Note

1 Johnson, S. M. (2019). *Attachment theory in practice: Emotionally focused therapy with individuals, couples and families.* New York, NY: The Guilford Press.

Index

abandonment: anxious attachment 17; by attachment figures 56; attachment trauma 16; borderline personality disorder 66, 67–68; narcissism 62, 63, 64; referring out 54; by therapist 59, 97
abuse 33, 35–36, 55, 56, 61, 80, 94–95
adaptive behaviors/strategies 12, 57, 68, 76, 88, 90
addiction 74–85
adrenaline 19, 90, 98
adverse childhood experiences 54–55, 80
aggressive clients 86–104
amygdala 9–10, 112
analgesia 78
anger 21, 46, 64, 66, 69, 86–104, 108
anxious (hyper-activating) attachment 15, 16, 17
arousal states, heightened 13
attachment 6–24; ability to regulate emotion 8–9; and addiction 76–81, 84; and anger 91; anxious (hyper-activating) attachment 15, 16, 17; attachment distress 8; attachment trauma 16, 56–58, 65, 67; avoidant (de-activating) attachment 15, 16, 17–18, 20, 21, 55, 62, 81; basics of 7–9; biological nature of attachment 10; bonds with therapist 27; borderline personality disorder 65, 67; child attachment experiences 7, 15, 76, 81–82, 83; client blocks in therapy 45, 49; corrective attachment experiences 55; disorganized attachment 16–17, 56, 58, 65, 68; emotional regulation 7, 8–9, 15; Emotionally Focused Therapy 30; Greek mythology 61; as integrated neurobiological system 9–14; myths 20–21; and narcissism 61–62; personal lives 106; and personality disorder 54, 65, 70; quality of attachment bonds 8, 15; science of 6–24; secure attachment 15–23, 55, 58; understanding human behavior 7, 8–9, 14, 30; violence in relationships 95; *see also* insecure attachment
attunement 4, 15, 30, 44
authority figures 107–109
autonomy 16, 20
avoidance strategies 29
avoidant (de-activating) attachment 15, 16, 17–18, 20, 21, 55, 62, 81

behavior modification approaches 14
belonging 37
biological nature of attachment 10

Index

"black and white" thinking 57–58
blocks: client blocks in therapy
    42–43, 45–48;
    countertransference 35–38; to
    empathy generally 28–29; going
    around instead of addressing 47;
    personality disorder 58–60;
    therapists' 35–38, 43–44, 49,
    58–60, 65
borderline personality disorder 53,
    54, 56, 65–70
boundaries 4, 14, 22, 39
Bowlby, Dr John 7, 20
Bowlby, Richard 7, 20
brain reward centers 77
Brown, Brené 25, 52, 54

caregiving relationships 8, 15, 17,
    56, 65
child attachment 7, 15, 76,
    81–82, 83
childhood trauma/adverse
    experiences 54–55, 80
"clinginess" 18, 21
coaching 47, 48
Coan, Jim 19
co-creation of reality 31
codependency 20, 21
cognitive empathy 14, 26, 27,
    48, 71
comfort zone 34
coming alongside clients 35; see
    also leaning in
Common Factors theory 32–33
compassion 26, 28
compulsive behaviors 76, 78
congruence 43, 44, 105
connection: and addiction 78,
    80–81, 84; and anger 89, 91–92;
    and attachment 16, 17, 20,
    21–22, 30, 31; as basis of
    emotional safety 48; coping with
    distress 45; definitions of
    empathy 27; disconnection
    12, 13, 78, 102; as the help
    for dysfunction 23; humans
    hardwired for 105;
    interdependency 71; and
    the nervous system 19, 28,
    40; online 112–113;
    physiological effects 19; survival
    mechanisms 88; therapeutic
    alliance 26, 27, 32–35, 44, 46,
    49, 71; therapist as instrument
    of 44
control, seeking 14, 22, 66–67, 76,
    79, 90, 94, 95
coping strategies 9, 16, 53, 58, 77
co-regulation 13, 15–16, 71, 95
cortisol 19
countertransference 35–38, 39,
    49, 65
couples therapy: addiction 78;
    angry/hostile clients 86; client
    blocks in therapy 47;
    Emotionally Focused Therapy
    106; personality disorder 59, 68,
    70; therapeutic alliance 32–33;
    violence in relationships 93–96
criminal behaviors 15, 23, 36–37
curiosity 46, 48, 97, 99

danger cues 10–11, 93, 96
de-activation 63
de-escalation 95
defenses: addiction 76, 84; anger
    90, 98–99; client blocks in
    therapy 35, 46; handing to client
    60, 71; personality disorder 58,
    66, 68–69, 71; resistance 29;
    therapists' 33, 69, 87
denial 78–79
dependence 20, 21
depression 22
despair 89–90
destabilization 45
diagnosis 2–3, 52–53
disconnection 12, 13, 78, 102
disintegration of emotional
    signals 14
disorganized attachment 16–17,
    56, 58, 65, 68
Dissociative Identity Disorder 56
distance, emotional 18, 44, 48,
    62–63, 90
domestic violence 94
dopamine 19, 77
double trauma 57

Index

drained, being 38–40
drugs/alcohol 74–85
DSM (Diagnostic and Statistical Manual of Mental Disorders) 3, 55, 61, 66
dysregulation 45, 65, 66, 86, 97

early attachment experiences 76, 81–82, 83
echo chambers, emotional 39–40
Eliot, George 105
emotional avoidance 71
emotional cut-off 62–63
emotional distance 18, 44, 48, 62–63, 90
emotional draining 38–40
emotional muscle memory 26, 27, 39
emotional neglect 80
emotional presence 18–19, 27, 28; *see also* leaning in
emotional regulation: addiction 76, 84; attachment 7, 8–9, 15; client blocks in therapy 45; co-regulation 13, 15–16, 71, 95; personality disorder 65
emotional safety: angry/hostile clients 100; authority figures 109; client blocks in therapy 45, 48; countertransference 36; and empathy 27, 28, 33; personal lives 105, 106; personality disorder 59, 60, 64, 71; social media 111
emotional swords 35
emotional understanding 26
Emotionally Focused Therapy 3, 4, 7, 26, 30, 34, 59–60, 71, 106
emotionlessness, appearance of 31–32
emotions, emotions 11–12
empathy, definition of 25–29
environment scanning 10, 12
ethical guidelines 34, 43
euphoria 77, 80–81
experiential working 48, 71

Facebook 106–107, 111–113
faking empathy 40

fear 17, 28, 66–67, 87, 88, 93, 96
fight/flight/freeze 8–9, 11, 12, 13, 30, 87, 88, 106
fMRI scans 8, 12
forgiveness 38
Freud, Sigmund 2
frontal cortex 9, 96

grandiosity 61, 63
groundedness 59, 114
gut feelings 13

healing your own wounds 29
heard, feeling 30, 33, 87, 88, 97–98
hope 89–90
hormones 19, 28, 77, 90
hostile clients 86–104
humanity, seeing people's 36, 75–76, 109, 113
hyper-activating (anxious) attachment 15, 16, 17

impulsivity 66
inconsistent caregivers 15, 56, 65
independence 20, 21
information signals 12, 14, 30, 31, 49, 97
inner peace 79
insecure attachment: addiction 75, 79, 81; attachment science 8, 15–20; narcissism 65; personality disorder 54, 57–58, 64; violence in relationships 95
interdependency 20, 71
interpersonal neurobiology 12–13
interventions 30
intimate partner violence 94

Johnson, Susan M. 4, 6, 7, 42, 86
judgment: block to empathy 32, 33, 38, 43, 48, 54; labels of 3–4; narcissism 62; "personality disorder" 52–53; in therapy 30; violence in relationships 93–95

Kohut, Heinz 26, 27

Index

labelling 3–4, 53
lack of empathy 60–61, 62
leaning in: to anger 88, 92, 96–100; co-creation of reality 31; couples therapy 33; resistance 45, 46; therapists' blocks 4, 33, 44, 48, 87; to therapists' own anger 101–102
leaving relationships, advice to 4, 52, 61, 93
limbic system 9–10, 96
loneliness 22, 78, 79, 82
lovable, seeing oneself as 8, 55, 99
love 42, 54, 55, 68–69, 77

Matè, Gabor 16, 55, 74
meaning-making 10–11
medical model of mental health 2–3, 14, 53, 75
medication 14, 75
mentors 49, 101, 107–108
mirror neurons 39–40
muscle memory, emotional 26, 27, 39

narcissism 4, 53, 54, 60–65, 70–71
narcissistic personality disorder 56
neglect 55, 56, 57, 80
nervous system: addiction 76–77; anger 96, 97; attachment science 10, 11–12, 15–16, 19; fear 67; perceptions of reality 31; survival instincts 30
neuroception 11–12
neurological brain imaging 8, 12
neuroplasticity 8
neurosis 53
norepinephrine 90
numbing 12, 31, 62, 65, 71, 76, 80

over-repairing 17
oxytocin 19, 77

pain aversion 114
pain management strategies 17, 19, 79–80, 87, 93, 96, 99–100
pathologization: of addiction 74; behavior modification approaches 14; gets in the way of seeing humanity 36; narcissism 62; of one partner in a couple 33; overcoming resistance 46; "personality disorder" 3, 52–53; of resistance 29, 43, 48; therapist resistance 42, 44
perception 31
persecution 63
personal biases 43
personal lives, relentless empathy in 105–115
personality disorder 3–4, 6–24, 29–30, 52–73
physical pain 10, 12
physiological effects 19
plasticity 27
politics 111–112
potent relationships 7
present, being 7, 15, 27–29, 38, 46, 48–49
primary attachment figures 7–8, 15; *see also* caregiving relationships
professional mentors 49, 101, 107–108
projection 2–3
prosody 40, 91
psychiatry, history of 2
psychopathy 15, 61
psychosis 53
psychotherapy: Emotionally Focused Therapy 3, 4, 7, 26, 30, 34, 59–60, 71, 106; and empathy 26; history of 2

quality of attachment bonds 8, 15

randomness 30
reactivity: anger 87–88, 90, 92–93, 98; borderline personality disorder 69; narcissism 64; personality disorder 53, 54, 58, 59, 60, 66, 69, 106; resistant clients 43, 48, 49; social media 111
reality, perception as 31
reciprocity 7, 15, 18
referring out 2, 34, 54

Index

reflection 27
refusing clients 34
rejection: anger felt as 88; anxious attachment 17; by attachment figures 56; attachment trauma 16; borderline personality disorder 67–68; narcissism 62, 63, 64; physical pain of 10; referring out 54; by therapist 54, 59; of therapists' efforts 70, 97
relapsing 75, 84
relational coping 13, 34
relational survival 9
relationship-building skills 28
renewability of empathy 40
repairs 97, 109
resilience 15, 55, 84
resistance 29–32, 42–51
resonating chamber, being a 27
reward centers 77
rigid thinking 59–60, 63, 66
Rogers, Carl 34
romantic partners 7–8, 55, 66, 77–78; see also couples therapy

safe havens 22, 27, 45, 100; see also emotional safety
Sanderfer, Kenny 15
secondary emotion 59, 89
secure attachment 15–23, 55, 58
secure base 19, 22
seen, feeling 27–28, 36, 101, 111
self of the therapist issues 43, 44, 49
self-awareness 30
self-esteem 43, 61, 83
self-love 62–63
self-regulation 76
self-reliance, compulsive 18, 56
self-soothing 16
self-worth 15, 83
sensory information 31
separation anxiety 18–19
serotonin 19
sexual abuse 56, 57, 81, 82–83
shame 34, 83, 94
Siegel, Dan 24n11, 41n7
situational couple violence (SCV) 94, 95
skillsets, clients outside your 34
smothering 17
social media 111–113
soldiers 88
splitting 56, 57
sponge vs. the mirror 38–40
stressful situations 15, 19, 28, 76, 77
subjectivity 31
substance abuse 36–37, 74–85
supervision 34, 49
survival instincts 7, 9, 11, 30
survival mechanisms: addiction 76; attachment 10–11, 13; connection 88; fight/flight/freeze 8–9, 11, 12, 13, 30, 87, 88, 106; narcissism 63, 64; numbing 12, 31; personality disorder 58, 60; separation anxiety 19
sympathy 14, 25–26, 27

theories of resistance 2
therapeutic alliance 26, 27, 32–35, 44, 46, 49, 71
therapist resistance 43–44
Thoreau, Henry David 25
threat responses: anger 87–88, 90, 91, 92–93; fight/flight/freeze 8–9, 11, 12, 13, 30, 87, 88, 106; neurology 11–12, 112; personality disorder 66, 67; therapists' 109
threat-detection systems 10–11
tone of voice/prosody 40, 91
trauma 16, 17, 43, 55–58, 76, 80, 83
triggers: addiction 75; resistance 47; therapists' 48–49, 58–60, 69, 86, 92, 97
trust 21, 45, 49, 55, 57, 64, 66

unconditional positive regard 34
unprocessed trauma 43
unresolved wounds, therapists' 43

vasopressin 77
violence in relationships 93–96
violent clients 35–36, 37
vocal prosody 40, 91

vulnerability 63, 64, 70–71, 72, 84, 85, 89, 96

walking the talk/congruence 43, 44, 105

windows of tolerance 33, 40, 71, 96, 98–99, 102, 103
withdrawal 11, 86, 91, 92
workaholism 81–82
workplaces 110–111

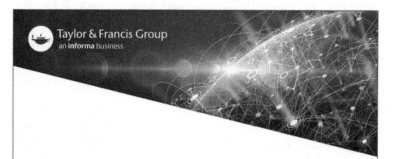